D0278713

ELDERLY CARE MEDICINE

Cavendish
Publishing
Limited

London • Sydney

TITLES IN THE SERIES

ELDERLY CARE MEDICINE

Dr Gurcharan S Rai, MD, MSc, FRCP
Consultant Physician in Geriatric Medicine,
The Whittington Hospital, London
Regional Advisor in Geriatric Medicine, North Thames (East)
Honorary Secretary of the Section of Geriatrics and Gerontology,
Royal Society of Medicine

Dr Stephen Webster, MA, MD, FRCP
Consultant Physician in Geriatric Medicine, Addenbrooke's NHS Trust
Honorary Associate Lecturer, Faculty of Clinical Medicine, University of Cambridge

**SERIES EDITOR
Dr Walter Scott, LLB (Hons),
MBBS, MRCGP, DObstRCOG**

Cavendish
Publishing
Limited

London • Sydney

First published in Great Britain 2000 by Cavendish Publishing Limited, The Glass House, Wharton Street, London WC1X 9PX, United Kingdom

Telephone: +44 (0) 20 7278 8000   Facsimile: +44 (0) 20 7278 8080

E-mail: info@cavendishpublishing.com

Visit our Home Page on http://www.cavendishpublishing.com

British Library Cataloguing in Publication Data

Rai, Gurcharan
Elderly care medicine – (Medico-legal practitioner series)
1 Aged – Medical care – Law and legislation – Great Britain
I Title II Webster, Stephen
344.4'1'0326

ISBN 1 85941 529 6

Printed and bound in Great Britain

FOREWORD

When I first conceived the idea of the *Medico-Legal Practitioner Series* in the summer of 1994, I had been preparing reports for lawyers on cases of alleged medical negligence for about five years. I had also been looking at other doctors' reports for the same length of time and it was becoming increasingly apparent to me that one of the lawyers' most difficult tasks was to understand the medical principles clearly. To be fair to the lawyers, there were some doctors who did not always make matters very clear. This, coupled with the difficulty which many doctors have in understanding the legal concept of negligence and related topics, merely served to compound the problem.

More than three years have now passed since I wrote the foreword for the initial launch of the series and, already, the number of titles available in the series has reached double figures with many more imminent. Therefore, this seems to be an appropriate moment to take stock of our efforts so far and to assess the way in which matters are likely to unfold in the future.

Since the publication of the first books in the series, there have been some exciting developments in the medico-legal scene and there can be no doubt that this is becoming an increasingly specialised field. That trend is likely to continue with the establishment of legal aid franchise firms of lawyers. Such firms will find it more and more necessary to identify strong cases and eliminate weak ones in an economical fashion and with as little risk as possible.

One important feature of the more recent titles in the series is the inclusion of case studies which are placed adjacent to the relevant parts of the text and are listed in a table for ease of reference. Most chapters have several examples of cases which have either settled in the plaintiff's favour or have fallen away because, perhaps, they were considered to be weak on negligence or causation. These studies give the reader a 'feel' for the work of the clinician and the difficulties which face him. The patient's expectations do not always correlate particularly well with the doctor's treatment plan, for example, in relation to consent, and such issues as this are often highlighted by the case studies.

The other interesting development in some of the newer titles is the coverage of areas that do not relate to clinical negligence. With the series becoming more comprehensive, we have felt able to expand into other medico-legal areas. Examples include *Respiratory Disorders* which deals with industrial lung disease and *Psychiatry* which covers testamentary capacity and the defence of insanity to criminal charges.

So much, then, for the latest developments in the *Medico-Legal Practitioner Series*. Our aim remains as it was at the outset with regard to uniformity of approach and clarity of presentation. In this way, I hope that our readers, mostly the practitioners who are engaged in unravelling the complexities of the medical evidence that is the subject of so much litigation, will continue to rely on us as an invaluable source of reference.

Walter Scott

Series Editor

Slough

ACKNOWLEDGMENTS

Grateful acknowledgment is made for permission to use extracts from the following:

Coni, N, Davison, W and Webster, S, *Lecture Notes on Geriatrics*, 1st edn, 1977, Blackwell Scientific;

Lueckenotte, AG, *Pocket Guide to Gerontologic Assessment*, 1990, CV Mosby.

Grateful acknowledgment is made to the Office of National Statistics for permission to use extracts from English Life Tables; to the NHS Centre for Reviews and Dissemination, University of York, for extracts from the Effective Health Care Bulletin; to Elsevier Science for extracts from Trends Endocrinol Metab; and to Robinson Healthcare, Walton, Chesterfield.

Every effort has been made to trace all the copyright holders, but if any have been inadvertently overlooked, the publishers will be pleased to make the necessary arrangements at the first opportunity.

CONTENTS

Contents

Contents

Contents

TABLE OF CASES

TABLE OF FIGURES

TABLE OF ABBREVIATIONS

ABR ....age-based rationing
ACE ....angiotensin-converting enzyme
AD ....advance directive
AMPS...assessment of motor and process skills
AMTS ....abbreviated mental test score

BMA..British Medical Association
BMD ....bone mineral density
BPH ....benign prostatic hypertrophy

CPR ....cardiopulmonary resuscitation
CT scan ....computerised tomographic scan
CVA ....cerebrovascular accident

DADL ....domestic activities of daily living
DEXA ....dual energy x-ray absorptiontry
DGH ....district general hospital
DHS...dynamic hip screws
DNR...do not resuscitate

ECG ....electrocardiogram
EEG ....electroencephalogram
ECT ....electro convulsive therapy
ESR...erythrocyte sedimentation rate

FHSA ....Family Health Service Authority
FICSIT ....Frailty and Injuries: Co-operative
Studies of Intervention Techniques

GP..general practitioner

HONK ....hyper-osmolar non-ketotic coma
HRT ....hormone replacement therapy

IADL...instrumental activities of daily living

JIP ....Joint Investment Plan

MRI ....magnetic resonance imaging
MTS...mental test score

NG...nasogastric
NICE...National Institute for Clinical Excellence

PACTS ....Parilamentary Advisory Committee on Transport and Safety
PADL ....personal activities of daily living
PSA ....prostatic specific antigen
PTSD ....post-traumatic stress disorder
PVS ....persistent vegetative state

ROM..range of movement
RTA ....road traffic accident

SAH...subarachnoid haemorrhage
SD ....standard deviation
SERM ....selective estrogen receptor modulator
SSRI...selective serotonin re-uptake inhibitor

T4 ....thyroxine
TIA ....transient ischaemic attack
TSH..thyroid stimulating hormone

WHO ....World Health Organisation

CHAPTER 1

DISEASE PRESENTATION/ILLNESS IN OLD AGE

Clinicians who care for older people have often noted that sick elderly patients may not present in the same way as younger persons. Such well known differences include the following points.

COMMON ILLNESSES TEND TO HAVE UNCOMMON PRESENTATIONS

Symptoms and signs classically associated with certain illnesses may be absent. Myocardial infarction, which usually presents with severe central chest pain radiating down the left arm or into the jaw, may produce a fall or shortness of breath in an older person. Unless this is appreciated and assessment, including an ECG, is performed by the physician, diagnosis will be missed. A peptic ulcer, when it ruptures, usually leads to peritonitis (inflammation of the peritoneum), and the patient has acute abdominal pain with rigidity and rebound tenderness (the pain increases when a doctor lifts the patient's hand while examining the abdomen). An elderly person with a perforation may have none of these features; the perforation may be detected some time later as an incidental finding on a chest x-ray performed for a suspected chest infection.

NON-SPECIFIC SIGNS AND SYMPTOMS

These are often the only evidence of a serious illness developing in old age. The four most common non-specific features, known as the 'giants of geriatric medicine', include confusion or intellectual failure, falls, immobility and urine incontinence. These modes of presentation of illness are common in old age. Once again, a simple and classical example is pneumonia, which may present with an acute confusional state (delirium) or fall, and only be diagnosed when a doctor carries out a thorough examination of the chest.

A young person with thyrotoxicosis (overactive thyroid gland) is likely to have a goitre (enlarged thyroid gland), exophthalmos (prominent popping eyes), agitation, increased sweating and palpitations. An elderly person with this condition may have none of these textbook clinical features; in fact, they may appear to be depressed or have features suggestive of an underactive thyroid gland.

CASE OF PULMONARY TUBERCULOSIS PRESENTING IN AN ATYPICAL MANNER

Figure 1.1   Chest x-ray showing changes of miliary tuberculosis

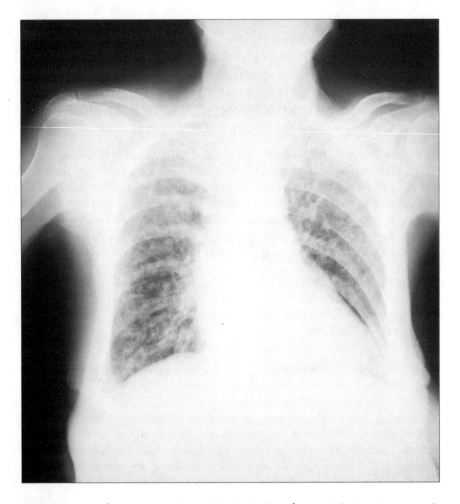

Figure 1.1 is a chest x-ray of an elderly lady who was living in a warden controlled flat. She came to the notice of her warden because she had stopped cleaning her flat. The patient herself denied having any symptoms. Her GP requested a domicillary visit from a consultant physician in geriatric medicine; he noted abnormal signs in the chest and ordered investigations, including an x-ray of her chest. These revealed miliary shadowing consistent with tuberculosis. As a condition, tuberculosis will lead to weight loss, general malaise, cough with sputum and shortness of breath. This elderly

person had none of these features. Staff of the sheltered accommodation were alarmed by the diagnosis and accused the GP of placing them at risk of acquiring a serious infection. The GP arranged for the staff to meet the specialist and, after talking to him, the staff dropped their complaint against the GP.

Serious illnesses may be mistakenly ascribed to changes associated with old age

This may be done not only by the individual and by his carers, but also by primary care physicians. 'It is just my age' is commonly reported by the individual and doctors may themselves falsely attribute aches and pains, fatigue and difficulty in walking, which can be part and parcel of a serious treatable illness, to an ageing process.

A single illness, such as influenza, can lead to catastrophic consequences

Influenza in a young person is likely to produce headaches, muscular aches and pains, temperature and a cough. With symptomatic treatment, the person gets better within a few days. However, in an older person, influenza may lead to:

- pneumonia, which, in turn, can lead to death;
- pneumonia, leading to atrial fibrillation (a fast, irregular pulse, which may lead to stroke and death);
- a fall, leading to a fractured neck of the femur, which can lead to immobility or death;
- confusion, which can lead to fall, immobility, contractures and pressure sores, requiring nursing care.

Figure 1.2   A single illness can lead to catastrophic consequences in the elderly

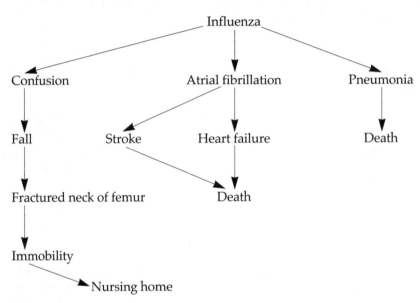

Multiple pathologies

Whereas a young person is likely to have a single medical problem on presentation to a doctor, an elderly person is likely to have multiple pathologies; one consequence of this is that symptoms and signs of a new disease may be wrongly attributed to the chronic old illness. For example, a patient with osteoarthritis may fall and fracture his femur, but the pain caused by the fracture may be attributed wrongly to the osteoarthritis.

These features make the medicine of old age challenging, requiring a high index of suspicion and a thorough assessment to identify the active pathology responsible for any non-specific features.

Case 1: pneumonia leading to a fall and a fractured neck of the femur

Facts of case

A 94 year old woman, who was very disabled as a result of multiple illnesses, including dementia, ischaemic heart disease, cerebrovascular accident and cataracts, required respite care admission on a regular basis. During one of her respite care admissions, she was left unsupervised during the nurses' tea break. The patient walked out of the dayroom, slipped and fell, fracturing her left femur, which required a transfer to a nearby district general hospital for surgical treatment. At the time of the fall and fracture, she had pyrexia (temperature of 38.5°C), a pulse of 120 per minute and basal crackles in the chest, that is, signs of a chest infection. This was not diagnosed until after she had been referred to the Accident and Emergency department.

Allegations made by the family

It was alleged by the family that the hospital staff had been negligent in leaving her unsupervised.

Expert opinion

The expert's report highlighted that, as the patient had pneumonia at the time of the fall, it was likely that the fall was a result of it and, therefore, negligence should be addressed in terms of the hospital (providing respite care) failing to detect the pneumonia and treat it.

Outcome

The case was settled out of court, with the hospital agreeing to pay a sum to the family.

Comment

This patient sadly passed away within six weeks of surgery, highlighting the increased mortality associated with a fractured neck of the femur.

Case 2: missed diagnosis of hypercalcaemia (high calcium), causing depression

Facts of case

An 84 year old woman was referred to a psychiatrist with a two to three month history of becoming weepy and requiring coaxing to eat and drink. She also had delusions of being dirty and infecting other people, her waste blocking drains and being a burden to her family. She expressed the idea of being better off dead, without being actively suicidal. A consultant psychiatrist made a diagnosis of psychotic depression and recommended fluoxitine and stelazine, as well as admission to hospital for assessment and observation. The patient had routine investigations. As she was not improving on drug therapy, ECT (electro convulsive therapy) was ordered. The patient had three courses of ECT before an anaesthetist noted that the patient's medical records contained a laboratory result highlighting a high serum calcium.

Two months later, she was seen by a physician who arranged admission for urgent treatment of her high calcium and its complication of dehydration and further investigations. While she was being investigated, the physician in charge of her clinical care informed the family that the patient had cancer, although he had no objective evidence of this. Subsequent results, in fact, confirmed that she had primary hyperparathyroidism, which was treated successfully with parathyroidectomy.

Allegations made by the family

The family complained to the hospital about the care received by their elderly relative. The independent consultants, who were called in to investigate the complaint, agreed that:

(a) a serious mistake had been made by the delay in action being taken by the doctors (on the psychiatric unit) following the high calcium result;

(b) the physician who investigated the high calcium at the second hospital should not have informed the family about the possibility of cancer causing the high calcium, but should have outlined all the possible causes.

Expert opinion

The medical expert appointed by the family's solicitors agreed with the conclusions of the independent consultants and further highlighted the point that the doctors failed to appreciate the fact that the high calcium can cause psychotic illness. Had they realised this, they might have prevented unnecessary prolonged suffering, symptoms of depression and unnecessary ECT treatment.

Outcome

The hospital accepted liability for the delay in checking the result of high calcium and for suffering inflicted on the patient. As a result of this negligence, they agreed to pay the family. The case was settled out of court.

Comments

This case highlights:

(a) the failure of doctors to appreciate presentation of a particular illness, that is, high calcium causing psychiatric symptoms;

(b) the doctor's failure to see the results of investigation he had ordered and to act upon them;

(c) the doctor's inadequate communication with the family by failing to tell them about the range of causes of high calcium.

Case 3: failure to diagnose heart failure

Facts of case

An 81 year old woman, with a past history of depression, hysterectomy, schizoid personality, gall stones, diverticular disease and congestive cardiac failure, was seen by her GP with vomiting, diarrhoea and weakness. On examination, the GP noted mild dehydration, a regular pulse of 76 per minute and blood pressure of 130/80 mm Hg. A chest examination revealed no signs, but an abdominal examination revealed slight tenderness in the right upper quadrant. The GP started her on codeine for diarrhoea.

Two days later, the GP was called because the patient had not improved. On this occasion, he noted that she had a markedly high respiratory rate but, once again, no signs were noted in the chest. The GP referred her to hospital for assessment, but by the time she arrived, she had no cardiac output. The patient was pronounced dead after resuscitation failed. A post-mortem examination recorded the cause of death as congestive cardiac failure and gastroenteritis.

Allegations made by the family

The family alleged negligence on the part of the GP for failing to diagnose and treat their relative appropriately.

Expert opinion

The expert's report on causation and, in particular, whether appropriate management of the elderly patient would have resulted in a different conclusion, highlighted the fact that the GP failed to diagnose congestive cardiac failure, because he did not appreciate:

(a) it may not present typically in some elderly people – while most patients with congestive cardiac failure have breathlessness, worsened by exertion, paroxysmal nocturnal dyspnoea (being woken by shortness of breath at night) and leg swelling, some elderly patients may have atypical symptoms, such as weakness, tiredness, fatigue or confusion;

(b) chest signs of fine basal crepitations, noted in patients with congestive cardiac failure, may not be audible.

Outcome

After reading the report, the family accepted the fact that an illness such as heart failure may not be obvious to a doctor. They did not pursue it further.

CHAPTER 2

FALLS IN THE ELDERLY

INTRODUCTION

A fall may be defined as where a patient has inadvertently come to rest on the ground or other lower level, with or without the loss of consciousness (PROFET Study (1999) 353 Lancet 93, pp 93–97).

Falling is by far the most important cause of hospitalisation for older people (see Figure 2.1). It is a leading cause of death from injury among people aged over 75; mortality caused by accidents and falls far exceeds that caused by pneumonia, diabetes or any other disease in older people. Looking at mortality figures for accidents, deaths from falls are far greater than the number of deaths due to road traffic accidents (RTA) or fire (see Figure 2.2).

Figure 2.1   **Age-specific hospital admission rates for falls among residents of South Thames (East) in 1991–92 (from Cryer, C, Davidson, L and Styles, C, *Injury Epidemiology in the South East: Identifying Priorities for Action*, 1993, South Thames Regional Health Authority)**

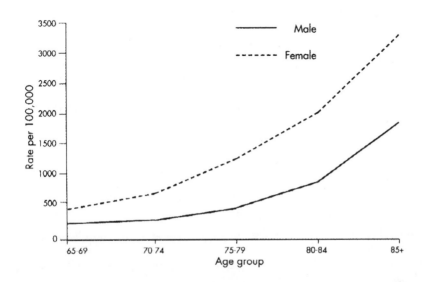

Figure 2.2 **Age-specific mortality rates from accidents among older people (OPCS mortality statistics, 1992)**

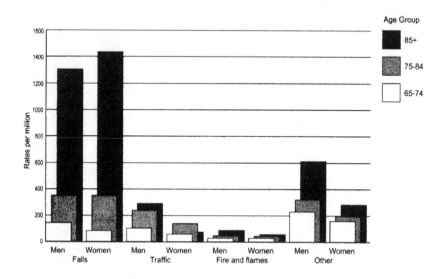

Each year, 30% of people over the age of 65 years living in the community fall, and the proportion of fallers increases with age.

The pathological basis of falls is diverse and complex, ranging from accidents due to environmental factors to physiological changes of ageing, illnesses/problems of muscles, joints, the heart or the brain and drug therapy.

PHYSIOLOGICAL CHANGES THAT INCREASE THE SUSCEPTIBILITY OF ELDERLY PEOPLE TO FALL

The physiological changes that increase the risks of falling include reduced muscle strength, increased body sway, slower psychomotor responses, poorer proprioception (position sense) and slower visual accommodation reflexes.

To maintain an erect posture requires balancing a very large mass with a high centre of gravity over a small base. This fine balance is maintained by the anti-gravity muscles, with input from the skin, muscles and joints, as well as from the eyes and vestibular (labyrinthine) function. Changes with ageing affect these reflexes, resulting in increased sway.

In 1963, Sheldon studied postural control by looking at sway and demonstrated (see Figure 2.3) that the skill of postural control is acquired in early years and remains with us until the age of 60, when it starts to deteriorate, the pattern at 80 years resembling that of a child. He studied postural sway by fastening an aluminium frame on the subject's shoulders, and had projecting from it a triangular piece with a spring loaded pencil at the apex. The subject was asked to stand still, with the pencil resting on a piece of graph paper at a suitable height. The main objective of the study was to measure how much the pencil moved or deviated from its original resting position while the subject was standing still for one minute.

Figure 2.3   **Effect of age on sway (from Sheldon, JH, 'The effect of age on the control of sway' (1963) 5 Gerontol Clin 129, pp 129–38 (Basel))**

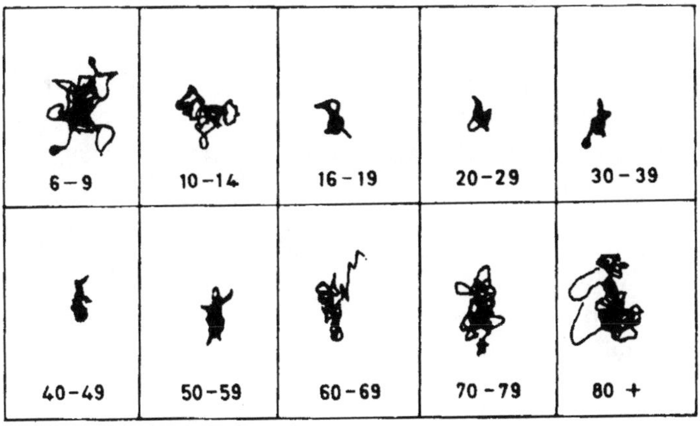

Cardiovascular disease

Cardiac arrhythmias

Irregular fast or slow pulse.

Silent myocardial infarction

Myocardial infarction or coronary artery thrombosis presenting without chest pain.

Postural or orthostatic hypotension (fall in blood pressure on standing)

Two elements of postural or orthostatic hypotension are a fall in blood pressure on assuming the upright posture and development of symptoms such as syncope or faintness. It is a common condition, occurring in 4% of the total population and 14–33% of the entire elderly population.

The pathophysiological basis of orthostatic hypotension is complex, but the key elements include the control mechanisms of resistance vessels through the sympathetic nervous system (this causes the arteries to constrict or narrow) and arginine oxide system (vasodilating system). With ageing, there are changes in these systems, which reduce the ability of the elderly to maintain blood pressure in response to changes in posture, thus making them liable to develop symptoms. The response to posture is influenced by the presence of illness or precipitating situations, such as the taking of certain drugs, for example, diuretics and anti-hypertensive agents. Treatment consists of using support stockings to improve venous blood return to the heart and removing the precipitatory drugs or situations. In some patients, symptoms improve with the use of fludrocortisone.

Carotid sinus hypersensitivity

In all individuals, a drop in blood pressure is first detected by the receptors located in the carotid sinus. Messages from these receptors go to the brain, which, in turn, influences the heart rate (by sending messages through the parasympathetic and sympathetic nervous system) and arteries to constrict, thus raising blood pressure. This is a normal response. With ageing, there is a change in the sensitivity of adenoreceptors in the heart and blood vessels. In addition, in some individuals, the carotid sinus receptors become hypersensitive and their response to fall in blood pressure is exaggerated. These individuals may develop falls or syncope as a result of low blood pressure or as a result of slowing of the heart rate.

Detection in sufferers can be easily achieved by performing carotid sinus massage for five seconds while measuring their blood pressure and monitoring their electrocardiogram (ECG). Those with carotid sinus hypersensitivity may have asystole (stopping of the heart) exceeding three seconds or a fall in systolic blood pressure to below 50 mm Hg. Those who exhibit a slowing of the heart rate can be treated successfully with a dual-chamber pacemaker.

Aortic stenosis

Narrowing of the aortic valve between the left ventricle and the aorta, which impedes blood flow in times of extra need, such as exertion.

OTHER KNOWN CAUSES OF FALLS

Acute illness

Premonitory falls may occur in the run up to an acute illness; it is estimated that they account for about 10% of falls unrelated to syncope.

Neurological problems

Transient ischaemic attacks, stroke, epilepsy and Parkinson's disease.

Drop attacks

These account for 10–25% of falls. The cause of drop attacks is unknown, but vertebro-basilar insufficiency (vertebro-basilar arteries supply blood to the hind brain, the cerebellum and occipital lobes; reduced blood flow through these arteries can lead to vertebro-basilar insufficiency), vestibular disorders and increased body sway have often been labelled as contributory factors.

Typically, a person standing in a kitchen whilst preparing a meal finds himself on the floor with utensils in his hand. There is no loss of consciousness, but the falling to the ground is associated with complete loss of tone in the muscles which maintain posture. The patient usually recovers quickly and is able to get up. Clinical examination often reveals no sequele.

Joint diseases

Examples include arthritis leading to unstable knee or hip joints and cervical spondylosis – arthritis affecting cervical spine (neck).

Muscle problems

Weakness due to low potassium levels, associated with hypothyroidism and muscle diseases.

Blood problems

Anaemia (low haemoglobin levels); hypoglycaemia (low blood sugar); hypokalaemia (low plasma potassium); and hyponatraemia (low sodium).

Eye problems

Poor vision from any eye disease.

Labyrinthitis

Inflammation of the labyrinth, which is a part of the inner ear involved in maintaining balance.

Alcohol

Alcohol leads to impairment of control over the trunk and legs, leading to characteristic staggering or drunken gait and increased liability to falls.

Micturition/defaecation syncope

Syncope is defined as a brief transient loss of consciousness, resulting from a temporary impairment of cerebral function. This leads to a loss of postural tone, but is recovered spontaneously, without intervention. In this condition, syncope develops during micturition or defaecation.

Drugs

Common drugs that may cause falls include diuretics, anti-hypertensives, drugs used for treating Parkinson's disease, sedatives, etc.

Environmental factors

Loose rugs, lack of bannisters, poor lighting, room cluttered with furniture, etc.

Elder abuse

See, also, Chapter 6. Elder abuse is common; a fall deliberately caused by a carer at home or a staff member in a nursing home has to be considered, particularly where abuse is suspected or has been diagnosed earlier.

RISK OF FALLING

While any one of the known causes listed above can lead to a fall, the risk in an individual will depend on the number of risk factors he has, the risk increasing with linearity as the number of factors rises. One study, examining the effect of risk factors in 336 persons over 75 years of age, noted that risk increased from 8% in those with one risk factor to nearly 80% in those with more than four risk factors.

PREVENTING FALLS AND SUBSEQUENT INJURIES

In the community, identification of risk factors has led to interventions to prevent falls in high risk patients. Interventions which have been evaluated include:

(a) the role of exercise;

(b) the role of home safety assessment by occupational therapists;

(c) identifying risk factors in institutions;

(d) the use of hip protectors;

(e) improving nutrition;

(f) rationalisation of medication.

Role of exercise

In America, exercise has been evaluated by the FICSIT trials (Frailty and Injuries: Co-operative Studies of Intervention Techniques). This evaluation of exercise involved seven sites over a three year period and over 2,400 volunteers. Most of these sites were in the community, but two were set in nursing homes.

Exercise programmes included flexibility training, resistance and/or endurance exercises, or dynamic training, using well known Chinese balancing exercises of Tai Chi. The pooled results of these seven studies suggest that exercise can reduce the risk of falling by 10%. However, a higher reduction was achieved by exercise programmes that included balance retraining. This was confirmed by a recently published study from New Zealand (Campbell, AJ, Robertson, MC, Gardner, MM, Norton, RN and Bucher, DM, 'Falls prevention over two years: a randomised controlled trial in women over 80 years and older' (1999) 28 Age and Ageing 513, pp 513–18).

Role of home assessment

The role of home assessment is to look at the environment. The falls can also be reduced by recommending a range of interventions or safety modifications or referral to care. Like exercise, intervention by a nurse advising on drug therapy or a physiotherapist providing instructions on gait and balance will reduce the risk of falling at home but, unfortunately, the benefit is not maintained if the intervention is discontinued.

Dietary intervention

Vitamin D not only affects bone, but has an important function in maintaining muscle strength. Deficiency can lead not only to bone loss or poor mineralisation of bone, but also to proximal muscle weakness. A recent systematic review, looking at vitamin D and calcium supplementation, noted reduction in fractures by 20% over a three year period with intervention. There is also some evidence that giving calcium alone may be effective in reducing symptomatic fractures.

Hip protectors

See, also, Chapter 7. Hip protectors are made of polypropolene, which allows energy from the fall to disperse away from the most vulnerable part of the femur, allowing it to be absorbed by the soft tissues and muscles surrounding the joint. While the wearing of hip protectors can reduce the incidence of fractures, they do not affect the risk of falling.

Use of restraints

Families often ask, and some insist, that their elderly relative in a home is restrained or observed 24 hours a day to prevent falls, ignoring the fact that their relative is an individual, who has the right to privacy and dignity, and that the basic principle of care for the elderly is to allow them to be independent and have control over their life. In addition, family members and/or carers do not appreciate the dangers of restraining elderly patients who are confused.

Results of a study involving 322 subjects in three nursing homes, where 119 were restrained and 203 never restrained during a nine and a half month period, showed that the restrained group was four times more likely to have falls or recurrent falls than the non-restrained group.

Consequences of falls

Apart from injuries, falls can lead to fear of falling and loss of confidence. As a result of this, an elderly person may restrict his activities, affecting his quality of life. To a certain extent, fear of falling and lack of confidence can be overcome with treatment.

MEDICO-LEGAL ASPECTS OF FALLS

Advice given to doctors

In the case of falls occurring outside the home or institution, action taken by an individual will depend upon the extent of injury. Fatal injury or death should be reported to the Coroner's Office. Other injuries should be referred to an Accident and Emergency department for full assessment – particularly to exclude fractures – and treatment.

Falls in hospital

Each hospital has an accident reporting policy. This will usually insist on a nurse completing an incident/accident form and a doctor examining the patient for the presence of injuries. As in the community, if a fall results in death immediately or follows treatment for injuries resulting from the fall, the doctor will refer the case to the Coroner.

Case 4: inappropriate use of cot-sides, leading to a fall and a fractured neck of the femur

Facts of case

An 84 year old man was admitted at 4.00 am with confusion. At the time of admission, he was agitated, had hallucinations (seeing insects crawling up the wall) and showed signs of pneumonia in the chest. The admitting doctor prescribed antibiotics and, when the patient arrived on the ward, nurses put him to bed with cot-sides to prevent him falling from the bed. They then went to complete nursing records for the daytime staff, leaving him alone. The patient, in his confused state, climbed over the cot-sides and fell, acquiring a fractured neck of the femur on the right side.

Allegations made by the family

The family complained to the hospital management about the poor standard of care it provided.

Outcome of discussions between family and hospital staff

Hospital managers organised a meeting between the relatives, consultant physician and the manager of the unit. At this conference, the management conceded the fact that the care they provided fell below the accepted standards. They accepted that:

(a) the nurses should not have used cot-sides, but should have allowed him to lie on a mattress on the floor;

(b) the nurses should have realised the risk of falling exhibited by patients with delirium (confusion) and should have ensured he was supervised closely.

Outcome

The family accepted the apology from the hospital and did not pursue the case further.

Case 5: confused patient, who was appropriately managed, fell and acquired a fracture of the elbow

Facts of case

An 85 year old lady was admitted with delirium (confusion), secondary to a urinary tract infection. This was treated appropriately with antibiotics. Within two days of treatment, the patient's confusion improved, although it did not completely resolve. By the third day, the patient was walking independently on the ward and decided that she wanted to go home, leaving the ward without the nurses' knowledge. Whilst walking, she fell outside the hospital and fractured her elbow, which required two surgical procedures. Despite this, the patient could not straighten her elbow.

Allegations made by the family

The family sued the hospital for negligence, stating that: (a) the hospital should have observed her 24 hours a day; (b) she should not have been allowed to walk by herself; and (c) had she been closely monitored, she would not have walked out of the hospital and would not have acquired the fracture.

Expert opinion

The expert witness for the patient agreed with the family that the hospital was negligent in allowing her to walk unsupervised.

The expert witness for the hospital highlighted that:

(a) it is not an acceptable practice to observe all patients 24 hours a day, especially when they are recovering from an acute illness;

(b) patients may not wish to have 24 hour supervision and may, in fact, feel threatened;

(c) part of the management of illness in old age is to allow elderly patients to regain independence, in anticipation of returning home.

Outcome

The judge ruled in favour of the hospital.

Comment

Delirium (confusion) is a common presentation of acute illnesses, such as pneumonia. During the agitated state, an individual may harm himself and, therefore, require nursing in a quiet, semi-dark room, with close monitoring. Occasionally, a patient may require constant supervision, known as 'specialing', for a period, but it must be remembered that a confused person may consider this threatening and may try to hit out and run away. The risk of this happening can be reduced by using a member of the family for supervision.

CHAPTER 3

INCONTINENCE

INCONTINENCE OF URINE

Prevalence

Incontinence is one of the common problems encountered in old age, but it is not a normal feature of ageing. Reported prevalence rates in the community are 10–20% for women aged 65 years and over and 7–10% for men aged 65 years and over. An even greater prevalence is noted in old people in residential homes (25–30%) and in nursing homes (50%).

Normal bladder anatomy and physiology of micturition

Anatomy of the normal lower urinary tract, concerned with micturition (passage of urine) is represented in Figures 3.1 and 3.2. The bladder acts as a storage for urine and is able to retain about 500 ml without leaking. The wall of the bladder has a series of stretch receptors. Stimulation of these receptors by the filling of the bladder results in impulses going to the sacral segments (S2, S3 and S4) of the spinal cord, which, in turn, sends impulses (messages) to the bladder muscles, causing it to contract. As the bladder muscle, known as detrusor muscle, contracts, the sphincters relax, allowing the flow of urine from the bladder into the urethra. In the resting normal state, the sphincters ensure that there is no leakage of urine.

In order to ensure that we micturate at an appropriate time and in an appropriate place, we develop voluntary inhibition of micturition (see Figure 3.2). This main control of the bladder and urethra is exerted through the descending fibres from the motor nuclei of the pons and medulla parts of the brain. Messages from this are able to produce sustained contraction of the bladder, while inhibiting the smooth and striated muscles of the sphincters. The working of these nuclei in turn is controlled by the micturition centre in the frontal lobe, which receives messages from the lower parts of the brain (pons and medulla) and the bladder itself, ensuring that micturition is co-ordinated, that is, that it takes place at an appropriate time and in an appropriate place.

Figure 3.1   Lower male and female urinary tracts

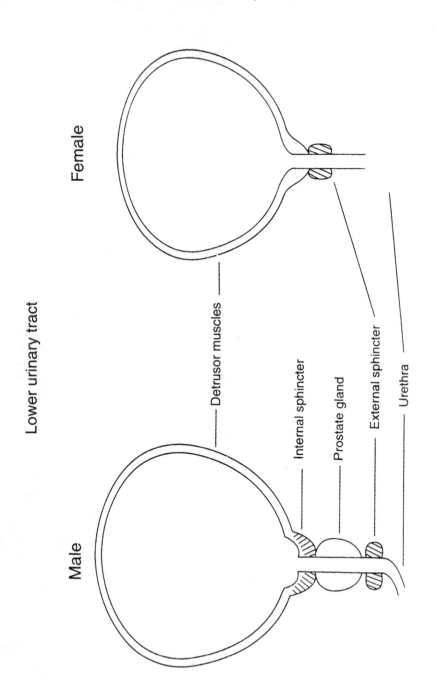

Figure 3.2   Neurological control of micturition

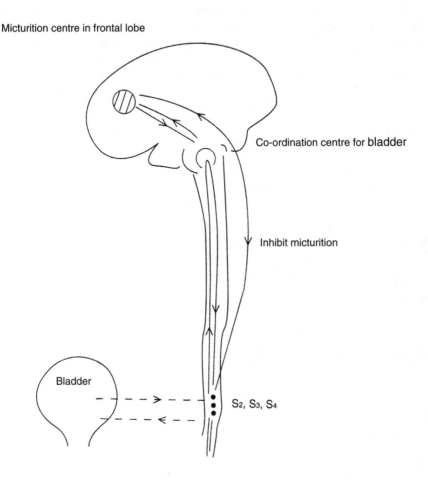

Micturition centre in frontal lobe

Co-ordination centre for bladder

Inhibit micturition

Bladder

S_2, S_3, S_4

Causes of urinary incontinence

Urinary incontinence can develop not only as a result of conditions or pathologies affecting the lower urinary tract, including the bladder and the nervous control of micturition, but also from non-bladder causes, such as the inability of an elderly person to get to the toilet in time, problem with transfers and the presence of confusion.

The common problems of the bladder that may lead to incontinence include its inability to accommodate a large volume of urine or the inability of bladder muscles to contract sufficiently at a convenient and appropriate time and place.

The urethra, which comes off the bladder, is able to maintain pressure above that in the bladder, thereby ensuring continence. During micturition, the smooth and striated muscle sphincters relax, lowering urethral resistance and allowing micturition. Any condition or pathology affecting the normal bladder or urethral function can and does lead to urinary incontinence.

Common treatable causes of urinary incontinence

The common treatable causes of urinary incontinence include:

* urinary tract infection;
* atrophic vaginitis;
* side effects of drugs such as diuretics, sedatives and non-steroidal anti-inflammatory drugs;
* drugs such as calcium channel blockers;
* reduced mobility;
* delirium – with confusion, the individual may not appreciate when and where to empty the bladder appropriately;
* depression;
* constipation/faecal impaction.

Other causes of urinary incontinence

Detrusor instability

This is a very common cause of established incontinence. The instability may be caused by obstruction, due to nerve fibres carrying inhibitory impulses, or idiopathic (aetiology unknown). Symptoms include frequency, nocturia, urgency and urge incontinence.

Bladder tumour or calculus (stone)

Stress incontinence

This is due to weakness of the pelvic floor and bladder neck muscles in women. This may result from damage to muscles during childbirth, or as a result of oestrogen deficiency or uterine prolapse and cystocoele.

Diagnosis can be made by examining the patient, who is standing with a full bladder, and asking her to cough.

Urinary retention with overflow

This is due to unsustained detrusor activity in response to obstruction and is the second most common cause of incontinence in men. Causes of this include prostatic hypertrophy, a loaded colon due to faeces, urethral stricture or a large mass (often a tumour) occupying the pelvis.

Neurogenic bladder

This results from damage to neural control of the bladder. Depending upon the lesion, different types of incontinence may result. These include the following.

Uninhibited bladder

With this type of incontinence, there is a loss of involuntary cerebral inhibition due to a stroke, Parkinson's disease, multi-infarct dementia or a frontal lobe tumour. With this, the individual will have complaints of urgency and frequency.

Reflex

Here, the individual has bladder detrusor hyperreflexia without sensation; therefore, the bladder empties when it fills to a certain volume; the sufferer is not aware of the incontinence. This often results after injury to the spinal cord.

Atonic

With atonic incontinence, there is detrusor areflexia with variable loss of sensation, depending upon the site of the lesion. Causes include diabetes mellitus, trauma from pelvic surgery and tabes dorsalis. Symptomatically, these patients have retention of urine with overflow (dribbling), with or without sensation. The typical symptoms are a recurrent urinary tract infection associated with high residual urine.

Assessment of patient with urinary incontinence

Clinical assessment, including accurate history and examination, is essential for defining the problem and its possible causes. Minimal examination should include an assessment of the person's mobility, mental state, an abdominal examination, a rectal examination to detect prostatic size (in men) and faecal impaction (constipation), a pelvic examination in women, a neurological examination looking at anal tone, perineal sensation and planter responses, post-residual urine volume measurement using a catheter or ultrasound (this provides information on how much urine may be left after a person has finished micturition, that is, how efficient a person is emptying the bladder) and a urine test, using a dipstick, for leucocytes and nitrites, which indicate the presence of a urinary tract infection.

In some selected individuals, it may be necessary to proceed to specific tests using urodynamic equipment, which measures flow rates, urine volumes, bladder filling and pressures during voiding.

Treatment of urinary incontinence

Treatment of common causes

Urinary tract infection

This requires appropriate antibiotic therapy – usually, a three day course. The choice of antibiotic will be determined by the sensitivity of the organism or bacteria producing the infection.

Faecal impaction

Treatment of constipation with suppositories, enemas and laxatives taken by mouth.

Atrophic vaginitis

Treatment with oestrogen cream applied locally or tablets taken by mouth.

Prostatic hypertrophy in men

Treatment includes surgery, laser treatment or selective alpha–1 blockers, such as alfuzosin and doxazosin. These drugs block the sympathetic nervous activity and, through this, relax the smooth muscle component of prostatic obstruction.

Stress incontinence

Pelvic floor exercises with or without biofeedback; electrical therapy and vaginal cones work in 'young' elderly patients. In others, surgery to strengthen pelvic muscles may be useful. Although there are a number of procedures that can be performed surgically for stress incontinence, there is no general agreement as to which is the best procedure. Recently, several devices have been developed to help patients with stress incontinence. The two forms of devices are: (a) the FemAssist, a device that covers the urethral orifice; and (b) Reliance, an intraurethral plug, which has to be removed each time the woman wishes to pass urine.

Bladder/detrusor instability

Bladder retraining works in some well motivated individuals. In others, imipramine, which is an anti-depressant, has anti-cholinergic action and, through this, may reduce urgency, increase intervals between bladder emptying and thus may result in independent or assisted continence. Other effective drugs include oxybutinin, which has anti-muscarinic action, and tolterodine, which has fewer side effects.

Some patients with incomplete emptying improve with intermittent self-catheterisation.

If all else fails, and the person does not have a treatable cause, then management of urinary incontinence consists of using pads and sheets or with permanent catheterisation, particularly if an older person is frail or has detrusor underactivity.

Conservative treatment of patients who fail to respond to treatment or those who have untreatable causes of urinary incontinence

Incontinence pads and sheets

These can be disposable or washable and vary in their absorbant properties and size.

External devices

Devices such as condom catheters/penile sheaths are useful for male patients. These can be self-adhesive or supplied with separate adhesive strips; unfortunately, they still have the tendency to fall off and are easily pulled off by confused persons.

Indwelling catheters

For short term use, a catheter made of latex is preferred, but those requiring catheterisation on a long term basis should have a silicone-coated catheter. Individuals in whom a catheter is placed temporarily should have the catheter clamped for two hours daily to retain bladder capacity. Complications of indwelling catheters include infection, encrustation leading to catheter blockage and bladder spasm. A catheter specimen of urine may produce mixed growth or significant growth of organisms on culture, but patients only require treatment with antibiotics if they have associated symptoms.

FAECAL INCONTINENCE

Faecal incontinence, one of the most distressing conditions, is said to occur in approximately 3% of elderly people living at home and in up to 23–45% of elderly people in continuing care beds. While age associated changes, such as dimunition in anal squeeze pressure and decrease in the distension of the rectum, which produces the desire to void, may predispose to faecal incontinence, there are specific conditions that lead to faecal incontinence. The common causes include:

- constipation/faecal impaction with overflow – the presence of hard faeces causes the mucosa to secrete mucus, which results in soiling by liquid or semi-solid faeces several times a day;
- diarrhoea from any cause, for example, infection, drugs (including laxative abuse) or irritable bowel syndrome;
- factors relating to access to the toilet;
- difficulty with mobility, so that an individual cannot get to the toilet in time;
- difficulty in removing clothes;
- rectal prolapse;
- carcinoma of the rectum;
- diverticular disease of the colon;
- inflammatory bowel disease, for example, ulcerative colitis or Crohn's disease;
- dementia – the person becomes incontinent because he cannot appreciate when and where he should void or because he cannot resist faeces entering the rectum following a mass peristalsis, which occurs after food has entered the stomach. This results from the stimulation of the gastro-colic reflex;
- problems with the anal sphincter.

Management

Management of elderly people with faecal incontinence includes identifying the cause or causes of faecal incontinence and their treatment. In the majority of cases, faecal incontinence is treatable or preventable. A small minority with intractable faecal incontinence will require appropriate protective clothing.

Recently, faecal collection bags, which can be placed around the anus using an adhesive tape, have been introduced. These are particularly useful for elderly patients who are immobile or have severe diarrhoea.

The other important aspect of faecal, as well as urinary, incontinence is odour control. Many deodorants are available to achieve this.

CHAPTER 4

PRESSURE SORES

DEFINITION

A pressure sore, also known as a bed sore, is an area of localised damage to the skin and underlying tissue. It has been defined as an area of skin and/or tissue discolouration or damage which persists after the removal of pressure and which is likely to be due to the effects of pressure on the tissues. The basic reason for damage to the skin and underlying tissue is deprivation of oxygen and nutrients. They usually occur over areas of bony prominence, such as the hips, heels and sacrum, or the base of the spine (see Figure 4.1).

Epidemiology

Pressure sores are common in the elderly. The prevalence rate (the proportion of people who have pressure sores at a given point in time) reported in published papers varies from 3% to over 60%, but the average rate is approximately 5–10%.

Causes of pressure sores

Four major factors that contribute to the development of pressure sores include the following:

(a) pressure – blood flow to the skin is achieved through capillaries and the mean pressure in these vessels is 25–32 mm Hg. Pressure higher than this will occlude them and, as a consequence, the skin and the surrounding tissues will become anoxic (deprived of oxygen) and die. The damage to skin will depend upon the degree of pressure applied, the length of time that the pressure is maintained and the general health of the skin;

(b) shearing and friction forces – when pressure is applied at an angle to the skin, the various layers of the skin move over one another, causing distortion. This is likely to occur when there is friction between the skin and bed sheets. As with pressure, the magnitude of shearing is as important as the duration. Shearing force is particularly important for skin damage over the heels and sacrum;

(c) moisture, damaging skin integrity;

(d) hypotension – that is, low blood pressure.

Figure 4.1 **Sites commonly affected by pressure sores (from Lueckenotte, AG, *Pocket Guide to Gerontologic Assessment*, 1990, CV Mosby, p 76)**

A – supine

B – lying on side

C – prone

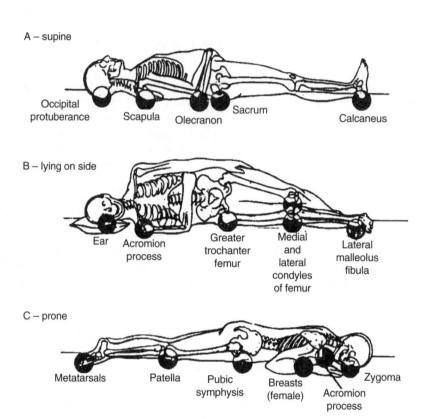

D – sitting

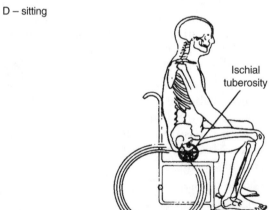

RISK FACTORS FOR DEVELOPMENT OF PRESSURE SORES

(a) Poor nutrition.

(b) Body type – very thin, malnourished people or obese people are predisposed to developing pressure sores.

(c) Immobility.

(d) Presence of acute illness, for example, anaemia.

(e) Urinary and/or faecal incontinence.

(f) Presence of neurological disease, for example, a stroke, Parkinson's disease or dementia.

(g) Presence of vascular factors, for example, diabetes and hypotension.

Nurses use various instruments and scales to quantify the risk, based on clinical variables, such as mobility, nutrition and incontinence. Two of the commonly used scales appear below.

Figure 4.2   Waterlow score (from Waterlow, J 'A risk assessment card' (1987) 83 Nursing Times 49, pp 49–55, revised March 1992)

Waterlow pressure sore risk assessment involves looking at build/weight for height, skin appearance, continence, mobility, sex/age and appetite, as well as special risk factors.

Build/weight for height		Visual skin type		Continence		Mobility		Sex/ Age		Appetite	
Average	0	Healthy	0	Complete	0	Fully mobile	0	Male	1	Average	0
Above average	1	Tissue paper	1	Occasional incontinence	1	Restricted/ difficult	1	Female	2	Poor	1
Obese	2	Dry	1	Catheter	2	Restless/ fidgety	2	14–49	1	Tube/ fluids only	2
Below average	3	Oedamatous	1	Incontinence of faeces	3	Apathetic	3	50–64	2	Anorexic	3
		Clammy	1	Doubly incontinent	3	Inert/ traction	4	65–74	3		
		Discolour	2					75–84	4		
		Broken spot	3			Chairbound	5	81+	5		

Special risk factors

1	Poor nutrition, for example, terminal cachexia	8
2	Cardiac failure	5
3	Peripheral vascular disease	5
4	Anaemia	2
5	Sensory deprivation, for example, diabetes, paraplegia, cerebrovascular accident	4–6
6	Orthopaedic surgery or fracture below waist	5

7	On table >two hours	5
8	High dose steroids, anti-inflammatory drugs or cytoxics in use	4
9	Smoking	1

Assessment value

At risk	10
High risk	15
Very high risk	20

Figure 4.3 **Norton score (from Norton, D, McLaren, R and Exton-Smith, AN, *Investigation of Geriatric Nursing Problems in Hospital*, 1962, National Corporation for the Care of Old People, re-issued 1975, Churchill Livingstone)**

Physical condition	Mental state	Activity	Mobility	Incontinent	Score
Good	Alert	Ambulent	Full	Not	4
Fair	Apathetic	With help	Slightly limited	Occasionally	3
Poor	Confused	Chairbound	Very limited	Usually	2
Very bad	Stuporose	Bedridden	Immobile	Doubly	1

Score of <14 – liable to develop pressure sores
Score of <12 – high risk of developing pressure sores

Although scales are used to evaluate the risk, there is little evidence-based data that proves that the use of risk scales results in a reduction in the incidence of pressure sores.

Assessment of sores

Assessment should include accurate documentation of pressure sores, including size, site and grade. The grading, listed below, provides information on tissue involvement, that is, whether it is confined to the top layer of the skin or deeper tissues.

Pressure sore grading

(See Figure 4.4.)

Grade 1   Erythema (skin is intact but discoloured).

Grade 2   Superficial break involving epidermis (top layer of the skin) and/or dermis (bottom layer of skin) – presents clinically as an abrasion, blister or shallow crater.

Grade 3   Dermis to deeper tissues – this involves full thickness skin loss with or without necrosis of underlying tissues.

Grade 4   Involves muscle/tendon/bone.

Figure 4.4 **Pressure ulcers in adults – prediction and prevention (from National Pressure Advisory Panel, 'Pressure ulcers in adults: prediction and prevention' (1992) 3 Clinical Practice Guideline (AHCPR))**

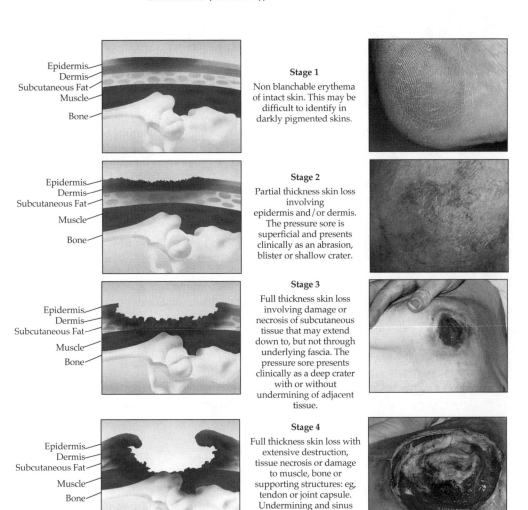

Stage 1

Non blanchable erythema of intact skin. This may be difficult to identify in darkly pigmented skins.

Stage 2

Partial thickness skin loss involving epidermis and/or dermis. The pressure sore is superficial and presents clinically as an abrasion, blister or shallow crater.

Stage 3

Full thickness skin loss involving damage or necrosis of subcutaneous tissue that may extend down to, but not through underlying fascia. The pressure sore presents clinically as a deep crater with or without undermining of adjacent tissue.

Stage 4

Full thickness skin loss with extensive destruction, tissue necrosis or damage to muscle, bone or supporting structures: eg, tendon or joint capsule. Undermining and sinus tracts may also be associated with stage 4 pressure sores.

Eschar
Accurate staging of the pressure sore is not possible until the eschar has been removed.

TREATMENT

General

General treatment consists of treating any other existing medical condition, correcting nutrition (supplements of vitamin C and zinc, which are known to improve wound healing, are sometimes prescribed), pain relief and physiotherapy to improve mobility.

Moist wound

There are many dressings available for pressure sores and examples of these include hydrocolloid for superficial granulating wounds and alginates for exuding or bleeding wounds.

In addition to dressings, surgical removal of dead tissue (debridement) may be carried out in appropriate patients.

Relief of pressure in those with established sores or those identified as at risk of developing pressure sores

Patients with established pressure sores or at risk of developing pressure sores will require the use of an appropriate support cushion for chair or mattress for bed.

Low risk patients

Low risk patients can be managed using a soft overlay or foam mattress and/or regular manual repositioning. However, there is little objective evidence showing that regular turning or repositioning prevents pressure sores.

High risk patients

Those at high risk of developing pressure sores will require large celled alternating pressure support system such as the Nimbus/Peagusus Airwave mattresses (containing alternating cells which are inflated and deflated by an electronically operated pump at seven to 10 minute intervals, so that the pressure on the body is continuously varied), water mattresses or net suspension beds (to aid repositioning).

Cost of pressure sores

Estimates suggest that a large district hospital will spend between £600,000 and £3 million per year.

Cost to patient

Apart from pain and suffering, patients with pressure sores have a fourfold increased risk of dying in hospital. The mortality is highest in those who develop bacteraemia or septicaemia from infected pressure sores.

Case 6: pressure sores developing after cerebrovascular accident – risk not assessed by nursing staff

Facts of case

Mr M, an 84 year old obese gentleman, was admitted after being found slumped by the side of his bed. On examination, he had left sided spastic weakness, left facial weakness and absent gag reflex. Based on his findings when admitting Mr M, the doctor concluded that the patient had a right hemispheric cerebrovascular accident and recommended intravenous fluids and nil by mouth until swallowing had been assessed by the speech and language therapist. In addition, he ordered appropriate baseline investigations, including a CT scan of the brain. The patient was admitted to a surgical ward, as there were no empty medical beds available in the hospital

On the same day (which was Friday), the speech and language therapist came to see the patient, but, as he was asleep and his posture was inappropriate, she could not carry out swallowing assessment and recommended to the staff that, if his posture improved, they should try to feed Mr M a spoonful of water – if coughing started, they should stop the trial and continue with non-oral feeding until Monday, when there would be a review.

On Saturday, Mr M was transferred to a medical ward. Nurses here noted that he had red heels (the beginning of pressure sores) and blisters on his sacrum. They carried out a risk assessment and recommended a ripple mattress and nasogastric (NG) feeding.

On Sunday, Mr M developed a chest infection, requiring intravenous antibiotics.

On Thursday, an NG tube was placed to start feeding.

Over the next four weeks, Mr M's condition deteriorated. His sores worsened, requiring surgical debridement. Despite starting parenteral feeding, Mr M deteriorated and died.

Allegations made by the family

The family were concerned about the standard of care received by their relative and consulted a solicitor, who requested an expert opinion on the care received by Mr M.

Expert opinion

In the medical report, the expert highlighted the areas of care where the hospital fell below the accepted standards and, in particular, pointed out that Mr M was at increased risk of developing pressure sores at the time of admission, but that no one on the surgical ward had assessed this risk until the pressure sores had developed.

Outcome

The hospital accepted liability for the inadequate standard of care resulting in pressure sores and settled the case out of court.

CHAPTER 5

CONFUSION (DELIRIUM, DEMENTIA AND DEPRESSION)

CONFUSION

'Confusion' is an imprecise term used by both the general public and health professionals to indicate disordered thought. The confused person may have difficulty with orientation and interpretation of reality, with the possibility of experiencing hallucinations and delusions. However, the patient is always fully conscious, often agitated, anxious and, sometimes, fully mobile. 'Delirium' is a medical term which describes the above situation.

Both delirium and confusion will be caused by an insult to the brain. This may be due to infection, by chemical changes, drugs, stress or damage to brain tissue or its circulation. Normal brains need big insults to cause problems, such as fulminating malaria in an otherwise fit young person or large doses of drugs (including alcohol). However, older people are more vulnerable, as they may no longer have the spare capacity or reserve they once enjoyed due to progressive and silent age changes in brain function and structure. For this reason, elderly people may become confused with very little provocation, for example, by a small dose of a drug, a mild infection or merely a change in environment and circumstances.

Confusion may be simply considered as a symptom of brain failure. This may be acute, that is, of sudden and unexpected onset, or chronic, that is, long standing. It may also be acute combined with chronic. In this third category, the person may function reasonably well in familiar and stable circumstances, but may be easily tipped into obvious confusion by a fairly minor precipitant.

DEMENTIA

'Dementia' is memory failure (usually, recent memory is more affected than distant) which, as a consequence, impairs insight and reasoning; consciousness is unaffected. In the early stages, motor function, that is, movements and activities, are unimpaired, but these do become damaged in time with the progression of the underlying disease process. A change in personality and a deterioration in personal standards and care are also a feature.

In dementia, brain tissue is damaged and altered. However, brain biopsies are not usually performed, so the diagnosis is usually made on clinical criteria. As a consequence, the accuracy rate is less than 100%. Dementia may be mistakenly diagnosed and differentiation into the various forms of dementia is also imprecise, as this too is made on clinical criteria.

The most useful tool in diagnosing dementia is the mental test score (MTS), but the abbreviated form of 10 questions (AMTS) is the most frequently used. More complex and time consuming test scores are available, but are usually only used by experts or in research settings. All the tests are fairly blunt instruments; they are of more value in documenting change in a clinical situation than in clarifying the diagnosis. A score of less than 70% of the total is usually an indication of the presence of dementia. Serious functional impairment is suggested by scores of less than 50%.

The problems beginning with 'D' which exaggerate an apparent degree of dementia are given in Figure 5.1. Conversely, some quite severely demented patients may function reasonably well whilst maintained in a familiar and stable environment. Self-assured and assertive people, as well as those with an ample and intact social veneer, can successfully conceal their problems; perhaps lawyers would fall into the first category and vicars' wives would be cited as examples of the other group!

Figure 5.1   Reasons for misleading low AMTS scores

Deafness: patient cannot hear questions.

Dysphasia: patient cannot understand questions and/or formulate a reply.

Drugs: patient too sedated to co-operate.

Delirium: patient too confused by acute problems.

Depression: patient too obtunded to co-operate.

Devilment: patient being provocative or mischievous.

When such people are stressed by change (both internal and external), their dementia may be unmasked. Close family members may be the last to appreciate a dementing process in a close relative. When the truth is revealed, for example, by admission to hospital, the loss of a spouse or a medical procedure, there is a temptation to blame the trigger as the cause, as the underlying problem (the dementing process) has progressed unnoticed.

The incidence of dementia

Dementia is not exclusive to old age. Those patients with early onset dementia – pre-senile dementia – are more likely than most to have an inherited form of the disease.

Cases of dementia increase in frequency with age, from about 5% in those aged 65 years to nearer 20% of people aged 85 years. Higher rates are found amongst the institutionalised, that is, residents in care homes. A rate of dementia in such homes is often in excess of 50%.

Other associations with dementia are:

- excess consumption of alcohol;
- malnutrition;
- repeated head injury, for example, in boxers;
- diseases that affect the vascular system, for example, hypertension, atherosclerosis and diabetes mellitus;
- chronic neurological disease, for example, epilepsy, multiple sclerosis and Parkinson's disease;
- genetic conditions, for example, Down syndrome;
- dialysis patients;
- infections, for example, syphilis, AIDS and encephalitis;
- raised intra-cranial pressure, for example, clots, tumours and hydrocephalus.

Types of dementia

Classification of dementia remains clinical and imprecise. However, the need to differentiate between types becomes more important as potential treatments become increasingly available.

Reversible dementia

This is a minority group of about 10% of all cases. However, their importance outweighs their frequency because of the opportunity to cure that they provide. The main sub-divisions are those cases due to deficiency states, for example, a lack of vitamin B12, folic acid and thyroxine, and those due to raised intra-cranial pressure, for example, clots, tumours and hydrocephalus. Diagnostic clues may be found in haematological or biochemical changes in the deficiency states, the presence of lateralising signs in the central nervous system and changes in the head CT in those secondary to raised intra-cranial pressure.

Alzheimer's disease

This is by far the most common type of dementia. It is slowly progressive over a period of about 10 years. It accounts for about two-thirds of all cases. If the brain tissues are examined, the abnormal proteins and structures described as plaques and tangles will be observed. Early onset cases may have a family history.

Treatments are now available for early, mild or moderate cases. The treatment enhances depleted levels of neurotransmitters (acetylcholine), but does not cure or reverse any changes and can only delay progression for about six months. Treatment is not freely available on the NHS – there is considerable geographical variation and, generally, prescribing is only permitted for psychogeriatricians, and then only with careful and detailed monitoring of clinical effectiveness.

Lewy body dementia is a subset of Alzheimer's disease. Its onset is slightly different, with the occurrence of more fluctuations in performance and the presence of hallucinations. The definite diagnosis can only be made by performing a biopsy, which is not clinically justified. Separation of this type is important, as sufferers react badly to phenothiazine drugs which are often used to control agitation and aggressive behaviour in demented patients.

Multi-infarct dementia

This accounts for about one-third of cases. It is usually associated with underlying vascular disease, for example, hypertension, atherosclerosis or diabetes mellitus. The vascular changes of narrowing of the lumen of the arteries and thrombosis lead to multiple small areas of destruction of the brain tissue. Each individual episode is likely to pass unnoticed, but, when considerable damage has accrued, the functional deficit becomes apparent. The deterioration occurs in a step wise manner.

The only therapeutic interventions are the early detection and control of the underlying diseases causing these vascular changes.

The course of the disease is generally shorter than that of Alzheimer's disease and the patient usually demonstrates physical disabilities, for example, mini strokes, as well as mental deterioration.

The consequences of dementia

- Acute toxic state.
- Inability to give informed consent and testamentary capacity.
- Lack of ability to co-operate with investigations and treatment.
- Risks of accidents and other illnesses.

Acute toxic state

This is the correct label to use when an elderly person, who was previously functioning well, is found to be in a confused state. The precipitating cause is usually an infection (especially a urine or chest infection, or a flu-like illness) or an infarction (myocardial or cerebral), that is, a silent heart attack or stroke. The episode is not actually silent, but merely talking to us in an unclassical presentation of disease (see Chapter 1).

The episode should be transient and should respond to antibiotic treatment if induced by a bacterial (not viral) infection. If it is due to an infarct, improvement should occur spontaneously, unless the damaged area is too great.

The patient's mind would appear normal, both before and after the acute toxic state. An MTS performed during the illness will be low, but will return to normal (or at least improve) on recovery. However, acute toxic states, if precipitated by a fairly mild insult, can be a harbinger of future dementia, the extra stress of the acute illness uncovering mild brain dysfunction that is too mild to be demonstrated on a simple MTS.

Such signs should alert the patient and their family to the danger of potential future problems. On recovery, the patient should be encouraged to make an enduring power of attorney and also an advanced directive (living will).

Informed consent and testamentary capacity

See Chapter 8.

Ability to co-operate with investigations and treatment

Severe dementia not only interferes with the ability to give consent, but will also impair the patient's ability to co-operate during investigations and during a post-operative period. Deficiencies in these activities are more restricting than the difficulty posed by the problem of consent.

Well-wishers may accuse medical attendants of denying a patient standard care because of their dementia, suggesting that the patient is being victimised because of their disease. However, it should be appreciated that it is empathy for the patient which will have dictated the approach to the patient and their problems. To expose a demented patient to a traumatic situation which they cannot comprehend is not only unkind, but also wasteful of resources, and the outcome (investigation results and therapeutic consequences) will be seriously sub-optimal. An alternative palliative approach is often the more humane route to take.

Enhanced risks of accidents and other illnesses

Because dementia removes insight, the afflicted patient is exposed to significant risks. These may comprise wandering in dangerous conditions, such as on main roads, in inclement weather or in inappropriate clothing.

Simple activities, which may still provide pleasure, may also acquire risks. Swallowing is often impaired in late dementia. This can expose the patient to the risk of aspiration pneumonia if food 'goes down the wrong way'. The patient will not be aware of or frightened by what might happen, but is still aware of the need to eat. A dietician, by guiding the patient towards safer foods, will reduce risks, but denying all food and using alternative methods of feeding will be abhorrent to the non-comprehending demented patient.

DEPRESSION

Depression is an important problem in old age, because:

- it is common;
- it is difficult to diagnose;
- it is treatable.

Incidence of depression

The incidence of the symptoms of depression are high in elderly people and tend to increase with ageing. However, there are many confounding factors which raise the level of depressive symptoms, such as poverty, isolation, illness and disability.

Ten to 20 per cent of the elderly have symptoms of depression, but this rises to 20–30% in those with acute illness and to over 30% in elderly people with chronic illness and disability.

Difficulties in diagnosis

First, depression is not always considered as an explanation for the poor functioning of a patient, or for a poor response to rehabilitation or other interventions. Often, symptoms are simply put down to age and thus dismissed. Secondly, the depression may only be one of several concurrent diagnoses and may be overlooked, as the others are more obvious and have more respectability, being more acceptable to both the patients and their families. Thirdly, depression may appear as something else, for example, early dementia, so the therapeutic openings available to depressed patients are not explored.

Treatment of depression

If the diagnosis of depression is made in old age, it should be treated. However, it has to be admitted that only one-third of patients respond dramatically to therapy. Treatment is also complicated by the intolerance of many frail, elderly patients to anti-depressant drugs. The newer drugs (selective serotonin re-uptake inhibitors (SSRIs)) are probably no more effective, but may be safer and have a lower risk of side effects. Electro convulsive therapy (ECT) has a mixed reputation but, in desperate circumstances, may be justified in the management of severe and potentially fatal cases.

Suicide, especially in elderly depressed men, is a very real risk and should be taken seriously. Unfortunately, many victims are only discovered after a successful action, which is more likely to have been of a violent nature than is found in younger depressed patients.

The social aspects of care of depressed elderly people also require active intervention. Unfortunately, the correction of poverty, social isolation and the occurrence of unpleasant life events are often beyond the resources of medical practitioners.

PARKINSON'S DISEASE

Parkinson's disease is a chronic, progressive neurological disease, caused by the impaired transmission of neurological messages between nerve endings. Its incidence rises with age, reaching one in 200 in those of pensionable age. The consequences of the disease are movement disorders, mainly tremor, motor rigidity and akinesia (difficulty in initiating spontaneous movements).

It has a slow and gradual onset; therefore, initial diagnosis is difficult and may be delayed. Most cases respond to treatment, usually with a form of the neurotransmitter L-dopa. However, the progress of the deterioration and degeneration is not terminated. The disease will progress relentlessly over many years. Also, the necessary increase in dosage of the required drugs also leads to toxicity. Although the quality of life is enhanced by treatment, the quantity may not be significantly increased and a stage of terminal dependence, as well as a need for palliative care, is usually unavoidable.

The onset of dementia in the later stages of the disease is usually the limiting factor in maintaining independence. Like all chronic diseases, Parkinson's disease may also be complicated by the onset of depression in about one-third of cases. Associated problems with postural control, bladder function and swallowing may also make drug treatment more complicated.

Parkinson's disease is a good example of a chronic degenerative neurological condition which impairs function and independence, but is also complicated by psychiatric complications. This lack of purity in the nature of the disease is very characteristic of geriatric practice.

Case 7: acute or chronic brain symptoms

Facts of case

An 84 year old woman was admitted to hospital in a confused state. Her GP had reported finding a right sided weakness, but this was not apparent on admission. There was, however, evidence of a urinary tract infection, and this was treated with antibiotics.

The patient improved, but not to her previously independent level of functioning. She developed mild signs of right sided weakness. At this stage (10 days after admission), a CT scan was requested and was performed two days later. The scan revealed an inoperable cerebral tumour.

Allegations made by the family

The patient's family complained that there was an unreasonable delay in making the diagnosis, which would not have occurred if a CT scan had been done on admission.

Expert opinion

On discussion with the family, it was explained that an acute toxic state was the most likely explanation for her confusion at the time of admission. However, when she failed to respond fully to the treatment of the urinary tract infection, other possibilities needed to be explored. It was at this stage that the CT scan was requested – to have done so previously could have been wasteful, as poor pictures might have been obtained as a result of the patient's agitation at that time.

The minor delay was not responsible for the inoperable nature of her lesion – that was due to its location and her other problems.

Outcome

The family withdrew their complaint after the explanation.

Case 8: son's inability to appreciate his mother's intellectual failure

Facts of case

A woman, who lived with her son, had suffered from Parkinson's disease for 15 years; it was clear from clinics and day hospital reports that her care in the community was precarious, even with her son's support.

Whilst in a care home, her condition deteriorated – she was admitted to hospital and died, having said to the son that she had been mistreated at the home.

Allegations made by the family

The woman's son complained that the patient was admitted to a care home against her will. He was due to be admitted to hospital himself and was the named main carer.

Expert opinion

An MTS had not been performed prior to the patient's final admission to hospital. However, after 15 years of Parkinson's disease, it was likely that she suffered from dementia and had clearly been confused during earlier acute illnesses.

Her GP records were poor and no notes were available from the care home. However, social services records showed that a full and proper assessment of her needs had been made by them prior to her admission to the care home. In addition, they had also reviewed her during her stay. There was also evidence from them that the son was an unreliable witness and had a severe alcohol problem. Moreover, there had been anxieties about his care of his mother when she was living in her own home.

Outcome

The case was dropped through lack of reliable evidence of neglect and admission to the care home against her will.

CHAPTER 6

ELDER ABUSE

INTRODUCTION

There is historical evidence of the abuse of elderly people by their family members as far back as the primitive nomadic tribes, who had the tendency to abandon their elderly relatives when they became a burden and could not sustain themselves. As an entity, old age abuse came to the notice of professionals in the 1980s and 1990s with the pioneering work of Eastman in 1984 (Eastman, M, *Old Age Abuse*, 2nd edn, 1994, Grosvenor (Age Concern)) and McCreadie in 1993 (McCreadie, C, 'From granny battering to elder abuse: a critique of UK writing 1975 to 1992' (1993) 5(2) Journal of Elder Abuse and Neglect 5, pp 5–23). Since then, many publications, based on research in the USA, Canada and the UK, have appeared, but, sadly, there is no agreement on a single definition of abuse.

DEFINITION

There are several definitions of abuse. Three of the most commonly used definitions are listed below.

Eastman's definition

Elder abuse is 'the physical, emotional and psychological abuse of an older person by a formal or informal carer. The abuse is repeated and is the violation of a person's human and civil rights by a person or persons who have power over the life of a dependent'.

Action on Elder Abuse's definition

This group, a registered charity, defines elder abuse as: 'A single or repeated act or lack of appropriate action, occurring within any relationship where there is an expectation of trust, which causes harm or distress to an older person.'

Definition produced in the 1993 Department of Health/Social Service Inspectorate guidance

This definition can be found in Department of Health/Social Services Inspectorate, *No Longer Afraid: The Safeguard of Older People in the Domestic Setting*, 1993, HMSO. It states that abuse may be described as physical, sexual, psychological or financial. It may be intentional, unintentional or the result of neglect. It causes harm to the older person, either temporarily or over a period of time.

Although multiple forms of abuse may occur in an ongoing relationship, for classification purposes, abuse has been divided into the following categories:

- physical abuse, for example, hitting, slapping, pushing, restraining or burning;
- psychological or emotional abuse, for example, swearing, shouting, blackmail, ignoring or humiliating a person or cultural intimidation;
- sexual abuse;
- neglect:
  (a) deprivation of nutrition, food, clothing or comfort;
  (b) involuntary isolation and confinement, that is, not allowing the individual to see or talk to others;
  (c) abuse of medications, that is, misusing medications, giving inappropriate drugs or not giving the prescribed drugs;
  (d) deprivation of performing activities of daily living;
- financial abuse, such as the illegal or unauthorised use of a person's property or money.

INCIDENCE/PREVALENCE

The true prevalence of abuse is not known, but estimates vary from 2% in the case of physical abuse to 5% for verbal abuse. These figures probably do not represent the true situation, since many elderly victims are not willing or are not able to admit abuse. In addition, there is often a reluctance on the part of professionals to identify and report abuse.

CHARACTERISTICS OF VICTIMS OF ABUSE

From the published data, primarily in the USA, it is possible to define the victim characteristics. Those who suffer from abuse are likely to be:

- female;
- over 75 years of age;
- afflicted by severe physical or mental impairment and, as a result, may be heavy, immobile and incontinent;
- living alone at home with an adult son or daughter;
- lonely, possibly with a negative personality trait.

Risk factors also include the presence of chronic progressive diseases, such as dementia, Parkinson's disease and severe cardiac or pulmonary disease. Other features may incorporate a personal history of violent behaviour or substance abuse, a history of child abuse, residing in an institution that has a history of providing substandard care or a sudden increase in stress in the carer as a result of the loss of a spouse or job.

Features of abuser

Research from the USA suggests that the abuser tends to be a son, who is likely to be dependent upon the victim for financial help, leading a stressful life, suffering from financial and health problems and possibly having a history of alcohol misuse and mental illness. While abuse which is physical and psychological is associated with the dependency of the abuser, psychological abuse is most likely to be associated with stress in the carer.

Manifestations of poor or inadequate care

Even when professionals have knowledge of the various facets of abuse, they might find it difficult to recognise, because some of the changes brought about by ageing, such as the thinning of skin, make elderly people bruise easily and such bruising may be difficult to distinguish from bruising due to physical abuse. Some workers have tried to prepare features that indicate poor or inadequate care (listed below), but it has to be remembered that the presence of some of these features does not necessarily establish the diagnosis.

Features of inadequate care

(Fumer, TT and O'Malley, TA, *Inadequate Care of the Elderly*, 1987, Springer.)

The presence of the following may indicate abuse:

- abrasions or lacerations;
- dehydration;
- contusions;
- inappropriate clothing or poor hygiene;

- burns or freezing;
- over-sedation;
- fractures;
- under-medication or over-medication;
- sprains or dislocations;
- untreated medical conditions;
- depression;
- pressure sores or skin ulcers;
- dangerous behaviour;
- finger marks;
- failure to meet legal obligations.

Other features suggestive of abuse

The patient may:
- try to hide his body;
- appear frightened, withdrawn, apathetic, anxious, aggressive or depressed;
- be afraid of a carer or a relative;
- be reluctant to be discharged;
- experience pain or itching in the genital area;
- have bloodstains on underclothing;
- be suffering from venereal disease;
- have bruising or bleeding around the genitalia or anus;
- have lost weight, have an unkempt appearance, be unshaven or be wearing dirty clothing.

PREVENTION AND TREATMENT

Interventions partly depend on the setting in which abuse has occurred and most social service departments, with or without input from local health authorities or hospitals, have guidelines on the management of suspected abuse. These may vary in detail from area to area, but most will have a policy of accurately recording all the circumstances of abuse, investigating them and ensuring that there is an agreed plan of action. The action may involve making arrangements to protect the elderly person at risk, including the possible involvement of the police where a crime has been committed.

While a case conference to discuss suspected abuse may recommend the removal of an individual from the place where abuse is being practised, this decision cannot be forced upon an individual who is mentally capable of making their own decisions. In the UK, there is no specific law covering elder abuse, although the Law Commission has made recommendations regarding an emergency assessment order.

The legislation under which local authorities are able to intervene in cases of suspected abuse is listed below.

Carers (Recognition and Services) Act 1995

This Act, which came into effect in April 1996, places a duty on local authority social services and social work departments to assess, on request, the ability of a carer to provide, and to continue to provide, care. This should be taken into account when deciding what services are required by a person in need of community care services.

National Health Service and Community Care Act 1990

This Act requires the local authority to carry out an assessment of need where an individual appears to require community care services.

Mental Health Act 1983

There are several parts of the Mental Health Act which can be used in cases of alleged or suspected abuse. These include the following.

Sections 2, 3 and 4

These can be used to admit to hospital a person who is suffering from a mental disorder, the severity and nature of which warrants detention in the interests of the individual's protection, safety or health.

Section 7

This allows the appointment of a local authority as 'guardian' to a person who has a mental disorder, including mental illness. The guardian has the power to require the individual to live at a particular place, to require access to be given to doctors, social workers and others at any place where the individual lives and to attend a particular place for treatment.

Section 115

Using this section, an approved social worker can enter and inspect premises of a person with a mental disorder if he has reasonable cause to believe that the person is not under proper care. Although this section does not give the power to enforce an entry, if the person refuses an approved social worker entry to his premises, he can be charged with an offence under s 129.

Section 135

Under this section, an approved social worker can apply to a magistrate to enter the premises with a police constable to remove a person, who is believed or considered to be suffering from a mental disorder, to a hospital or another place of safety for up to 72 hours. To use this section, the social worker must have reasonable cause to suspect that the person is suffering from a mental disorder and is being ill treated, neglected, kept in conditions other than under proper control or is unable to care for himself and is living alone.

Section 127

Under this section, it is an offence for staff of a hospital or a mental nursing home to wilfully neglect or ill treat a mentally ill patient who is subject to their guardianship or otherwise is in their custody of care.

National Assistance Act 1948

Using s 47 of this Act, the local authority can seek an order from a magistrate to remove an individual, who is considered to be at severe risk, from his home. Application for this must be supported by a certificate from a community physician, stating that the person is:

(a) suffering from a grave and chronic disease or, being aged, infirm or physically incapacitated, is living in insanitary conditions; and

(b) is unable to look after himself and is not receiving proper care and attention from others.

Registered Homes Act 1984

Under this Act, residential care homes are required to notify the Registration Authority (the local authority) of any event in the home which affects the well being of any resident and, specifically, of any serious injury to a person residing in the home. Using this Act, the local authority has the right to refuse registration to a home where there is evidence of institutional abuse and neglect.

Of course, if a person has committed acts such as theft, rape or assault as part of the abuse, they may be prosecuted in a criminal action or may have a civil action taken against them (for example, where the abuser's acts infringe upon the victim's property law rights or contravene family law).

Financial protection – the use of power of attorney and the court of protection

For a person who lacks sufficient mental capacity, social services can make an appointeeship, the duties of which will include claiming and using all State benefits on behalf of a person who is not able to manage his own affairs. In addition, a friend, spouse or relative can apply to the court of protection to appoint a receiver for the person.

A person who possesses the sufficient mental capacity can be advised to give power of attorney to another person they trust, in order to undertake transactions on the individual's behalf. Power of attorney is a deed whereby a person can grant another person the power of attorney, either on a short or a long term basis, to act on his behalf in financial matters. The power can be limited to a specific transaction or area, but it can also be granted as a general power.

Enduring Power of Attorney Act 1985

The Enduring Power of Attorney Act allows a person to appoint an attorney, who will continue to act on his behalf when he becomes mentally incapable. Once the attorney is aware that the individual who has appointed him has become mentally incapacitated, he must register his enduring power of attorney with the court of protection.

Case 9: institutional abuse

Facts of case

Mr A, who was 60 years old with progressive dementing illness, was placed in a nursing home, since his family could no longer meet his needs. During his time in the nursing home, Mr A became emaciated, his behaviour changed and, when he was admitted to hospital two years later, doctors noted signs of weight loss, dehydration, multiple grazes on his forehead, shins and forearms, discolouration of his toes, a greater trochanter (pressure sores) and a recent fracture of the pelvis. His wife and his daughter were so concerned by his state that they refused to allow him to return to the nursing home. Mr A was transferred to another health authority institution. The staff of the new home noted on admission Mr A to be 'desolate and dismal, showing apprehension of anyone'. With countless hours of tender loving care, he started to respond with a smile and verbal communication.

Allegations made by the family

The family instructed a solicitor to issue proceedings against the first nursing home for failing to provide suitable care and causing physical suffering.

Expert opinion

In his report, the expert highlighted the findings of the hospital doctors and, in particular, noted that the bruising, early pressure sores, fractures and weight loss are features that should alert professionals to the presence of abuse. In addition, he noted not only a weight loss of over five stones and a fall in serum albumin (an indicator of nutrition) during the time that Mr A was in the first nursing home, but an increase in weight and serum albumin after he had left the home.

Outcome

The case was settled by the defendants.

CHAPTER 7

HIP FRACTURES (FRACTURE OF THE FEMUR)

INTRODUCTION

The occurrence of hip fractures is rising in the world; in 1990, the estimated figure for hip fractures was 1.7 million and it is expected to reach 6.3 million by 2050, in line with the increase in the elderly population. In the UK, approximately 60,000 patients sustain a hip fracture each year; the majority of them are elderly.

The age specific incidence of fractures is increasing exponentially with age (see Figure 7.1). In women, 80% of fractures of the neck of the femur occur in those over the age of 70 years, whilst, in men, 50% of fractures of the neck of the femur are in those over the age of 70. The lifetime risk of fracture for a 50 year old is approximately 17.5% for women and 6% for men.

Figure 7.1   Incidence of hip, forearm and spinal fractures (from Cooper, C and Melton, LJ, 'Epidemiology of osteoporosis' (1992) 3 Trends Endocrinol Metab 224–29)

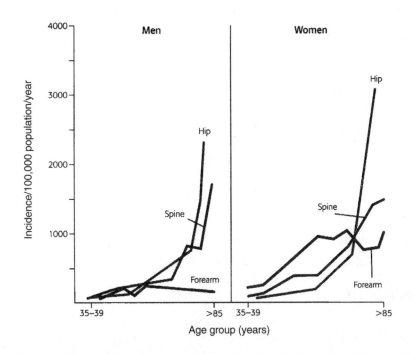

SEASONAL VARIATION IN RATE OF FRACTURE

In the UK, more fractures occur in winter months, especially during snowy and icy weather. While outdoor fracture rates peak in December and January, indoor fractures peak later, in March and April. Those who fall and sustain a fracture are likely to be malnourished and it is suggested that the high indoor fracture rate in March and April reflects the low vitamin D status which is a result of a lack of exposure to sunlight.

COSTS OF HIP FRACTURES TO THE NHS

Patients with hip fractures utilise 20–30% of all orthopaedic beds and, nationally, it is estimated that 4,000 NHS hospital beds are used in the management of fractures daily. Estimates for the cost of hospitalisation for a hip fracture lie between £2,230 and £6,200 (based on 1992–93 data). The average total cost of a hip fracture is over £12,300 and the estimate for the total costs of hip fractures to the UK is £840 million per year.

Costs to individual and their family

As a condition, a fracture is associated with increased morbidity and mortality. While three month mortality is 20%, this increases to nearly 35% by the end of a year following the hip fracture. The mortality associated with hip fractures increases with age, with the chances of survival being less in those over the age of 75 years, in men and in those who are in an institution at the time of the fracture. In addition, mortality increases year by year in survivors of a hip fracture; this stratified risk is not seen in elderly patients with other fractures. One follow up study has shown that only 26% of patients are alive 10 years after a fracture.

Of those who survive, 15–25% will be institutionalised and 25–30% will be more dependent; only 40% of those who were able to walk unaided prior to the fracture regain their independence after one year.

RISK FACTORS FOR HIP FRACTURES

A fractured neck of the femur may affect the following:
- the strength and intensity of bone – the major condition affecting the integrity of the bone is osteoporosis;
- the risk of falling;

- the direction of falls, that is, whether an individual falls forward, backwards or to their side. Those who fall to the side have a risk of sustaining a fracture 21 times higher than those who fall forwards or backwards;
- the effectiveness of protective neuromuscular responses to a fall;
- the energy of fall, which is determined by the weight of the individual and the distance he falls.

OSTEOPOROSIS AND HIP FRACTURES

'Osteoporosis' simply means thin bones (osteo – bone, poros – thin) and has been labelled as the 'silent epidemic'. The World Health Organisation (WHO) has defined osteoporosis as a bone mineral density (BMD) more than 2.5 standard deviations below the mean level for adults when assessed using dual energy x-ray absorptiomtry (DEXA – in this test, the differential absorption of two x-ray frequencies by bone and soft tissue is used to calculate the bone mass) or quantitative computer tomography. Although this is an arbitrary definition, it is useful in estimating the chance of a fracture in high risk patients. Fracture risk is always relative and increases progressively with decreasing BMD (about twice for every drop of one standard deviation). Standard deviation (SD) is a statistical term used to measure the scattering of observations – one SD above and below the mean includes 68% of the observations and two SDs above and below the mean includes 95% of normal observations.

As a test, a DEXA scan cannot be used to diagnose osteoporosis, because low values can occur in other bone conditions, such as osteomalacia (caused by vitamin D deficiency) or renal osteodystrophy (bone disease resulting from renal disease) and bone marrow disorders. In women reaching the menopause, the measurement is unfortunately not accurate enough to predict the risk of fractures 20–30 years in the future.

Causes of osteoporosis

Bone loss of ageing

With ageing, there is progressive bone loss; this accelerates in menopausal women and, by the time a woman reaches 90, her BMD would be approximately half the peak value. The mechanism for this accelerated decline is not clear, but oestrogen deficiency is a contributory factor. The higher the bone mass, the longer it will take the bone loss to reach a critical level at which fractures are more likely.

Other risk factors for osteoporosis

In addition to the bone loss of ageing, other known factors which lead to the development of osteoporosis include:

- female gender – part of the explanation for this is the difference in BMD, which is lower in women than in men;
- premature menopause;
- slim build;
- poor nutrition;
- sedentary lifestyle;
- long term use of drugs such as corticosteroids, anti-convulsants and warfarin – it is now recommended that those taking a dosage of corticosteroid of over 7.5 mg per day for a period of greater than six months should have risk factor assessment; this should include DEXA and being given calcium and vitamin D3, as well as an exercise programme. If, despite this, the patient continues to lose bone on the DEXA test, then he should be put on biphosphonate compounds, which not only prevent the development of osteoporosis, but also reduce the frequency of fractures;
- poor calcium intake;
- a family history of osteoporosis;
- smoking – the exact mechanism is not known, but it is thought that smoking produces osteoporosis through its action on oestrogen metabolism;
- thyrotoxicosis – an overactive thyroid gland;
- hyperparathyroidism – an over-production of hormone called 'parathormone' leads to the destruction of bone and a rise in blood calcium;
- heavy alcohol intake – alcoholics tend to have lower BMD and a rapid bone turnover.

Management of osteoporosis

Having identified these factors, doctors have tried to correct them by improving the bone mass and, therefore, reducing the likelihood of fractures in high risk patients. Interventions in high risk patients that have been shown to be effective include the following:

- Calcium, which is essential for the maintenance of the skeletal system; this has been shown to lead to a reduction of 30–40% in fracture risk.

- Calcium with vitamin D – this has been shown to reduce the incidence of hip fractures by 23%, and all fractures by 60%, after 36 months of treatment. This is particularly useful for elderly people who are housebound or who cannot get adequate calcium in their diet.

- Hormone replacement therapy (HRT) – this is not only useful in the prevention of osteoporosis, but also in the treatment of established osteoporosis; it is particularly good for post-menopausal women. In addition to arresting the reduction in BMD, HRT may reduce the incidence of fractures. The two questions that remain unanswered are:

  (a) is there accelerated loss of bone after HRT is stopped?; and

  (b) how long should the treatment be given?

- Selective estrogen receptor modulators (SERM), for example, raloxifene. These compounds mimic the action of oestrogen on certain organs, such as the bone, but not on other areas. Research so far has shown that raloxifene can increase bone density in the spine and hip. However, although it has been shown to reduce spinal fractures, there is little evidence at the present time on its ability to reduce hip fractures.

- Biphosphonate compounds, for example, etidronate (cyclical treatment with calcium) and alendronate. Alendronate has been shown not only to improve bone density, but also to reduce fracture risk in patients with osteoporosis. These compounds are useful in pre-menopausal women who develop osteoporosis, as well as post-menopausal women who cannot tolerate HRT or those in whom HRT is contraindicated and, of course, in men.

- Calcitonin – this is a hormone, produced by the thyroid gland, which inhibits or prevents the breakdown of bone. It has also been shown to reduce bone pain in patients with a crush fracture of the spine. Its major drawback is that the only form in which it is licensed for treatment of osteoporosis is as an injection.

- Prevention of falls (see Chapter 2).

- The wearing of hip protectors (see below).

- Exercise – in persons with established osteoporosis, exercise, especially weight bearing, is encouraged, in addition to specific therapy. Resistance exercise not only increases muscle strength, mobility and the ability to climb stairs, but may also result in a decrease in back pain and a trend to fewer further fractures.

Hip protectors

Hip protectors are made of polypropolene, which allows the energy to disperse away from the most vulnerable part of the femur, allowing it to be absorbed by the soft tissues and muscles surrounding the neck of the femur. In a controlled randomised study, hip protectors have been shown to reduce the risk of fracture by 53%, but, unfortunately, compliance by the very people who need to wear them is poor. A recent study of 97 patients in the community revealed a compliance rate of only 5%, the reasons for discontinuing hip protectors being discomfort and difficulty with toileting. In addition, it has to be appreciated that no one can force an individual to wear a garment if they do not wish to wear it. Then, of course, there is the ethical dilemma of imposing a hip protector on someone who has cognitive impairment and is unable to give consent.

DELAYED/MISSED DIAGNOSIS

It is difficult to miss a displaced fracture where the leg is shortened and lying in an externally rotated position. An undisplaced fracture is more difficult to recognise and may not be detected on x-rays, particularly if only one view is taken. This is the reason why it is recommended that radiographs should include a lateral view. In one study of 33 patients who had post-traumatic hip pain but negative x-rays, 40% had an intertrochanteric fracture confirmed on an MRI scan.

Reasons for missing diagnosis or for a delay in diagnosis include:

- an absence of pain or lack of symptoms in a stoic elderly person;
- elderly patients who are too confused to give a history of trauma or a history of symptoms;
- elderly people who are already dependent;
- spontaneous fractures, that is, fractures that occur without significant trauma.

HIP FRACTURES AND THEIR MANAGEMENT

Hip fractures (see Figure 7.2) are usually classified as extracapsular or tronchanteric (involving the intertronchanteric or subtrochanteric parts of the femur) or intracapsular or subcapital (involving the neck of the femur). The intracapsular fractures, which can be further subdivided into displaced subcapital or undisplaced subcapital fractures, may disrupt the blood supply to the femoral head and lead to osteonecrosis or non-union of the fracture. This is the reason for treating the displaced intracapsular fractures with femoral head replacement.

Figure 7.2   **Anatomy of the femur and hip joint, with sites of various fractures**

Anatomy of femur

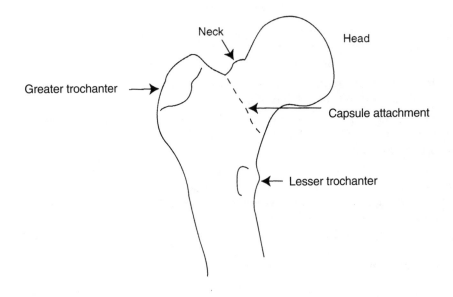

Neck

Head

Greater trochanter

Capsule attachment

Lesser trochanter

Types of fracture

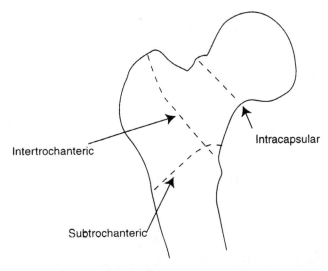

Intertrochanteric

Intracapsular

Subtrochanteric

Surgical management

Extracapsular (trochanteric) fracture

These fractures are treated by using sliding crew plates or intramedullary hip nails, such as dynamic hip screws (DHS) or intramedullary gamma nails.

Intracapsular fractures

The surgical treatment consists of hemiarthroplasty, where the damaged head of the femur is replaced by an artificial metal joint, which slots into the socket, and internal fixation for displaced and undisplaced fractures.

In terms of functional results, hemiarthroplasty or total hip replacement achieves better results than internal fixation.

Occasionally, a patient is so frail and confused as a result of dementia that surgery is not considered to be in his best interests; in such situations, prolonged traction may be recommended.

Early surgery, within 24 hours, by a dedicated surgical team if possible, unless the patient's medical condition precludes it, is considered desirable in order to reduce mortality and to prevent complications of bed rest, such as pressure sores, deep vein thrombosis, pneumonia and urinary tract infections. This was recommended as far back as 1989 by a working party of the Royal College of Physicians and there is now strong evidence that faster rehabilitation after a hip fracture can reduce the total care costs by 17%.

Early complications of hip surgery for fractures

First, patients with a fractured neck of the femur are at increased risk of developing chest infections, wound infections or urinary tract infections; therefore, most are given antibiotics as a prophylaxis.

Secondly, these patients are at high risk of developing thromboembolism (deep vein thrombosis and pulmonary embolism), with deep vein thrombosis incidence reaching 30%. Subcutaneous heparin is recommended as a prophylaxis. In addition to heparin, patients are encouraged to get on their feet within 24 hours.

Discharge from hospital following a fractured neck of the femur

Discharge will be dependent on the functional recovery made by the patient. This decision will be made by the multi-disciplinary team, with the involvement of the patient and his carers. Discharge back to the patient's home may involve:

- home visits from an occupational therapist, who will not only be able to give advice on getting rid of dangers in the home, such as loose carpets or rugs, but will also advise on details such as aids to assist the person around the house;
- advice from the physiotherapist on exercises to continue at home;
- personal care services, needed either on a temporary or permanent basis, in order for the person to remain in his home;
- further treatment, either at home or in a day hospital;
- treatment of any underlying conditions, such as osteoporosis, to reduce the chances of another fracture.

Case 10: delay in diagnosis of hip fracture

Facts of case

An 84 year old lady, who had a past history of osteoarthritis, asthma, osteoporosis and dementia, as well as a history of repeated falls, was sent to the Accident and Emergency department by her nursing home after she had tripped over a steel partition of a sliding door. At the department, she had x-rays of her pelvis and skull, which revealed no fractures.

Over the next few days, the patient continued to experience pain on walking and was re-examined by her GP on two occasions within five days of the fall. The first examination, which took place three days after the fall, revealed no signs of a fracture but, on re-examination on the fifth day, her GP noted that the patient's leg was shortened and externally rotated and referred her back to the hospital. On this occasion, the x-rays confirmed a displaced subcapital fracture of the neck of the right femur. The patient was seen by an orthopaedic surgeon, who recommended immediate surgery, but this had to be delayed because the anaesthetist feared that the patient may also have had subdural haematoma. Once the CT scan of the brain had excluded this, the patient had Austin Moore hemiarthroplasty on the fourth day, but sadly passed away two weeks later.

Allegations made by the family

The patient's family made a complaint against the nursing home staff and the hospital management for failing to diagnose the fracture earlier and causing unnecessary suffering.

Outcome

After discussions with hospital staff on the difficulty of detecting undisplaced fractures on x-rays, the family decided not to pursue the case.

Comments

- The fracture was missed by the first x-rays because:

   (a) only one view of the hip was performed; and

   (b) the fracture was not displaced.

- The family could have pursued this case successfully, because hospital staff should have taken x-rays of the hip in two different views.

- The patient's death within two weeks of surgery highlights the increased mortality associated with this condition, particularly in elderly patients who have co-existing illnesses.

Case 11: fracture not seen on plain x-rays revealed by bone scan

Facts of case

Figure 7.3 is an x-ray from an 85 year old woman who was referred to hospital after being found in a confused state by her home help. She displayed groin pain on examination, but there was no clear history of a fall. X-rays revealed no broken bones but, as the pain persisted, she had a bone scan (see Figure 7.4), which revealed an increased uptake of an isotope compound and, when the hip was x-rayed again, a fracture was visible (see Figure 7.5).

Figure 7.3   Normal x-ray of the femur

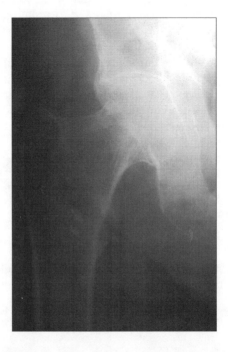

Figure 7.4   Isotope bone scan, showing an increased uptake in the region of the neck of the femur

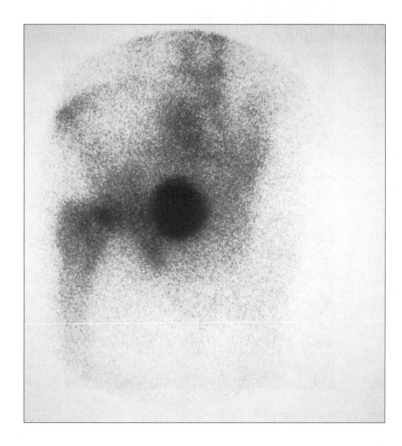

Figure 7.5   Displaced fracture of the neck of the femur

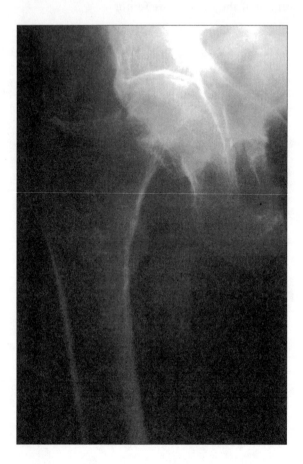

Outcome

Both the patient and her carer were given an explanation as to why an undisplaced fracture might not be seen on plain x-rays, but could be diagnosed on a bone scan. Both accepted the explanation and took no further action.

Case 12: delay in diagnosis of fracture

Facts of case

An 87 year old woman with a long history of depression, requiring several treatments with electro convulsive therapy, was admitted to a psychiatric hospital. The patient had a tendency to fall and records noted falls on several days during the first three weeks of her admission.

One week after admission, a physiotherapist noted that the patient had difficulty in walking. Two weeks later, a doctor noted that the patient was unable to weight bear. On examination, she displayed classical signs of a subcapital fracture of the femur. X-rays confirmed this and orthopaedic surgeons performed an Austin Moore prosthesis.

Allegations made by the family

The family alleged negligence in causing the fractured neck of the femur.

Expert opinion

In his report, the medical expert noted that the fracture either occurred spontaneously or as a result of a fall two weeks earlier and the patient could not weight bear when the fracture became displaced. As the patient was prone to repeated falls, the hospital could not be held responsible for the fracture.

Outcome

The family and their solicitor decided not to pursue the case.

CHAPTER 8

ETHICAL ISSUES IN THE CARE OF OLDER PEOPLE

INTRODUCTION

The issue of medical ethics is central to the sound practice of medicine of old age, in which ethical and moral dilemmas are commonly faced by doctors in the course of their everyday work. The difficult decisions and dilemmas commonly faced include withholding treatment, withholding fluids and nutrition, withdrawing treatment, the use of restraints, end of life decisions and resuscitation decisions in hospital.

When considering difficult dilemmas, the basic principles of medical ethics that doctors tend to rely upon include:

- autonomy – respecting patients' wishes and facilitating and encouraging their input into the medical decision making process. This includes elements of freedom from interference by others and the capacity for action;

- beneficence – this requires the doctor to act in the interests of the individual;

- non-maleficence – this principle places an obligation not to do harm to others.

MENTAL COMPETENCE

The Law Commission's test

This test states that:

> A person is mentally incapable if he is unable by reason of mental disability to make a decision for himself on the matter in question or he is unable to communicate his decision on that matter, because he is unconscious or for any other reason.

> A person is unable to make a decision if he is unable to understand the information (in broad terms and simple language) relevant to the decision, including information about the reasonably foreseeable consequences of deciding one way or another, of failing to make the decision or if he is unable to make a decision based on that information.

Assessment of mental capacity

In assessing mental capacity, it is important to realise that assessment is specific to the decision being undertaken. In an individual with mild impairment, assessment may involve:

(a) an examination of mental function, since problems with behaviour, memory, insight, cognition, language, mood, thought, perception and intelligence can affect mental competence;

(b) talking to other members of staff;

(c) talking to the family or friends of the individual.

In difficult cases, an independent medical practitioner, such as a psychogeriatrician, may have to be asked to see the individual.

In general terms, the law deals with the question 'is the patient mentally capable?' by answering on the balance of probabilities, that is, 'is it more probable than not that the person lacks the required mental capacity?'. This was one of the key recommendations made by the Law Commission (*Mental Incapacity – Item 9 of the Fourth Programme of Law Reform: Mentally Incapacitated Adults*, Law Com No 231, 1995). The other key recommendations included:

- a person should be regarded as unable to make a decision by reason of mental disability if the disability is such that, at the time when the decision needs to be made, he is unable to retain information about the reasonably foreseeable consequences of deciding one way or another, or of failing to make a decision;

- a person should not be regarded as unable to understand the information relevant to the decision if he is able to understand an explanation of that information in broad terms;

- a person should not be regarded as unable to communicate his decision unless all practicable steps to enable him to do so have been taken;

- a person should not be regarded as unable to make a decision by reason of mental disability merely because he makes a decision which would not be made by a person of ordinary prudence;

- any decision made on behalf of a person without mental capacity should be made in the best interests of that person.

Treatment of illness in patients who are not mentally competent

When a patient is not mentally competent, the doctor treating the patient makes the decision in his best interests. While the individual's next of kin or any other person has no right under English law to give or withhold consent for a mentally incapable adult, doctors often consult them and take their views into account when making the decision in the patient's best interests.

Having said this, the Lord Chancellor has recently proposed the establishment of continuing powers of attorney, so that people can give a trusted attorney the power to make decisions about their healthcare or welfare, as well as about their finances.

To help doctors in difficult cases, the Law Commission's report has given a list of factors which it feels doctors should consider when making a decision in the best interests of the patient, covering:

- the ascertainable past and present wishes and feelings of the person concerned, and the factors that person would consider if able to do so;
- the need to permit and encourage the person to participate, or to improve his ability to participate, as fully as possible in anything done for him and any decision affecting him;
- the views of other people whom it is appropriate and practicable to consult about the person's wishes and what would be in his best interests;
- whether the purpose for which any action or decision is required can be as effectively achieved in a manner less restrictive of the person's freedom of action.

Mental capacity and creating a will

In assessing testamentary capacity, doctors must ensure that patients know the nature of the action of making a will, have a reasonable grasp of their assets, know the person or persons to whom they are leaving their assets and are free of delusions which might distort their judgment.

For those who do not have testamentary capacity, doctors will recommend that the affairs of the patients are placed in the hands of the court of protection, unless enduring power of attorney was arranged before the loss of testamentary capacity.

AN ADVANCE DIRECTIVE OR LIVING WILL

An advance directive (AD) is a statement made in advance by a patient who is mentally competent at the time, stating his preferences for medical care and treatment if, at some stage in the future, he should become mentally incompetent. Although the Government has not produced legislation on this, the AD has become legally established in English common law under the following circumstances and conditions:

- the patient must have been competent at the time the AD was drawn up;
- the AD should clearly list the clinical circumstances under which he does not wish to receive treatment;
- the person must not have been under any duress when preparing the AD.

Although individuals can obtain a pre-printed AD from organisations such as the British Medical Association (BMA) or the Higgins Trust, they can prepare their own statements, ideally witnessed by a doctor, although this is not necessary.

ETHICAL DILEMMAS FACING DOCTORS REGARDING NUTRITION AND FLUID

Dilemmas often faced by doctors in relation to nutrition and fluid include:

- should we feed a particular elderly person?;
- should we stop feeding a particular person?

Before considering these two complex questions, it is important to remember that:

- nutrition and fluids are necessary for creating health, prolonging life and preventing illness;
- the law regards nutrition and fluid (hydration) as basic human requirements – non-provision to competent patients is unacceptable;
- methods of providing food and water by intravenous cannulae or nasogastric (NG) tube, however, fall under the heading of medical interventions;
- there is no legal or ethical distinction between withholding and withdrawing treatment.

The British Medical Association has just produced guidance (*Withholding and Withdrawing Life Prolonging Medical Treatment*, 1999) for decision making on the withholding or withdrawing of treatment by doctors. The guidance highlights that:

- the primary goal of medical treatment is to benefit the patient by restoring or maintaining the patient's health as far as possible, maximising benefit and minimising harm. If this cannot be achieved, then the justification for providing the treatment is removed;
- it is not an appropriate goal of medicine to prolong life at all costs, with no regard to its quality or the burdens of treatment.

Should we feed particular elderly people? Issues that a doctor has to consider when discussing such a question with other staff and the patient's family are:

- the preservation of life;
- the quality of life before the development of the illness;
- the quality of life after the illness has been treated;
- the patient's status in relation to pain and suffering.

Guidance from the BMA is that, where nutrition and hydration are provided by ordinary means, such as by cup, spoon or the moistening of a patient's mouth for comfort, this forms part of basic care and should not be withheld or withdrawn, certainly when there is a possibility that it will benefit the patient. However, this does not imply force feeding an individual – the person should be offered food, but should not be forced to take it. It should be remembered that a competent person has a right to refuse treatment and nutrition.

In the case of providing food and hydration by cannulae, NG tube or gastrostomy tube, procedures regarded as medical treatment, it is the duty of the doctor to ensure that the patient has all the information about the treatment, the consequences of not having the treatment and any other alternative forms available. A competent patient can refuse treatment and this refusal or advance refusal, left in the form of an AD, has to be respected by the doctors. In contrast to this situation, there is no obligation on the doctor to comply with an AD request for life prolonging treatment.

In the case of an individual who does not have the mental capacity to make decisions, the doctor in charge of the patient's care can make the decision, using the principle of the best interests of the patient.

Where treatment is withheld or withdrawn, the important facts to remember are listed below:

- there is no obligation on doctors to provide any treatment which is clearly contrary to an individual's health interest or where the patient is near death;

- before a decision is made to withhold or withdraw treatment, a thorough assessment by a multi-disciplinary team, with expertise in undertaking this type of assessment, should be carried out. The team should examine the benefits, risks and burdens of treatment in the particular case and, in addition, should take into account the views of people close to the patient, even though these views have no legal status;

- where a decision made by the clinician in overall charge of the patient's care is being challenged by others or where there is disagreement among the professionals providing the care, then a court review is advisable;

- in the case of patients in a persistent vegetative state (PVS) or in a state of very low awareness closely resembling PVS, it is an essential legal requirement to refer this to the court for review;

- where the patient is dying or his death is imminent, artificial nutrition and hydration may be withheld or withdrawn if it not considered to be of benefit to the patient.

Additionally, the BMA has recommended safeguards to doctors proposing to withhold or withdraw treatment in a patient who is not dying and whose wishes are not known. These are as follows:

- these proposals should be subject to a formal clinical review by a senior clinician who has experience of the condition from which the patient is suffering and who is not part of the treating team;
- all cases in which artificial feeding and hydration has been withdrawn should be available for clinical review to ensure that appropriate procedures and guidelines have been followed;
- anonymised information should also be available to the Secretary of State on request and, where applicable, to the commissioner for health improvement.

CARDIOPULMONARY RESUSCITATION

Resuscitation is regarded as medical treatment and, therefore, the same ethical and legal issues that apply to medical treatment in general apply to this too. Most hospitals have a resuscitation or 'do not resuscitate' (DNR) policy that is based on the guidelines issued by the BMA, in conjunction with the Royal College of Nursing. These guidelines recommend that:

- all DNR decisions should be clearly stated in the medical and nursing notes, without codes or medical abbreviations;
- the reasons behind the DNR decision should be recorded;
- junior doctors' decisions should be regularly reviewed by senior colleagues;
- the ultimate responsibility should rest with the consultant;
- the patient and, if appropriate, their next of kin should be involved in the decision, although discussion does not have to take place if a DNR order is made on grounds of medical futility.

Most policies recommend that a DNR order is appropriate under the following circumstances:

- where cardiopulmonary resuscitation (CPR) is not in accordance with the recorded and sustained wishes of the patient who is mentally competent. Refusal does not have to be specific to CPR – it can be implied by a repeated refusal of life sustaining or prolonging treatment by the patient;
- where the probability of survival is unlikely to be high;
- where the patient already has a poor quality of life and he does not wish to have his life prolonged. It is important to remember that this refers to *the patient's* view of his quality of life and not the view held by the doctors, who are known to underestimate the strength of feeling in patients.

In the case of a patient who is mentally incompetent to make decisions

DNR decisions once again can be applied on the grounds of futility, poor quality of life and the existence of a valid AD refusing resuscitation.

In other situations, doctors will discuss the benefits and risks of resuscitation with relatives, other professionals and carers, and then make a decision that is in the best interests of the patient.

The law and CPR decision making

- There is no specific law covering CPR.
- In the case of all medical treatment, a competent patient has a right to accept or refuse treatment.
- In the case of a patient who is mentally incompetent, the doctor bases his decision on the principle of the best interests of the patient.
- If and when CPR is considered to be futile, there is no legal requirement for doctors to discuss this with a competent person.

END OF LIFE DECISIONS

While considering moral and ethical decisions faced by doctors, it is important to consider the following definitions:

- *Euthanasia* – etymologically, the term 'euthanasia' is derived from the Greek words 'eu' and 'thanatos', meaning a 'good death'. However, a broader meaning now refers to the ending of a life of a person, for his own benefit, by another.
- *Voluntary euthanasia* – a deliberate and intentional hastening of death at the request of a seriously ill patient and through his own actions.
- *Involuntary euthanasia* – the ending of a person's life without seeking his opinion.
- *Non-voluntary euthanasia* – the ending of a person's life for his benefit, when that person cannot possess a point of view over whether he lives or not.
- *Assisted suicide* – a competent patient seeks help to commit suicide.
- *Physician assisted suicide* – the ending of a life of a competent patient by the consumption of a lethal cocktail of drugs prescribed by a physician.
- *Active euthanasia* – this implies an intention to hasten death, while *passive euthanasia* implies withholding or withdrawing active or curative treatment or life prolonging treatment.

Moral dilemmas faced at the end of life

Recently, three principles have been proposed to provide doctors with the tools to solve such dilemmas:

(a) the treatment of patients must reflect the inherent dignity of every person, irrespective of age, debility, dependence, race, colour or creed;

(b) decisions taken must value the person and accept human mortality; and

(c) actions taken must reflect the needs of the patient.

Thus, it is the duty of the doctor not only to have respect for the person in all aspects of medical management, but to ensure that his actions are of the highest standards. Included in this is the duty of the doctor to do no harm when preserving life. This, however, does not mean that the doctor must preserve life at all costs. When a medical treatment or intervention is no longer appropriate to sustain life or the means used to sustain life are out of proportion to the life achieved (that is, treatment is considered futile), death should be accepted and allowed to take its course.

In 1993, the House of Lords, on issues of life and death, ruled out legalisation on euthanasia, but accepted that the so called 'double effect' is an established part of medical practice, recognised in law. This means that, should it be necessary to relieve pain and suffering in a patient who is terminally ill, it is proper to give doses of analgesic drugs and/or sedatives of an adequate quantity to produce relief, even if that action has a secondary consequence of shortening life expectancy. In such cases, it is the doctor's intent which is crucial.

Decisions at this important time will also take into account:

- whether or not the person is competent to make decisions;
- whether the patient has left prior instructions in the form of an AD;
- whether a person has appointed an attorney to make clinical decisions on his behalf;
- the best interests of the patient.

USE OF RESTRAINTS

Published data suggests a high prevalence rate for the use of physical restraints in nursing homes, despite the lack of objective data showing its efficacy. In fact, empirical research data suggests that restrained individuals in nursing homes show more agitated behaviour and are more likely to suffer from constipation, incontinence, pressure sores and reduced functional capacity. They are also at increased risk of falls, especially those who have been restrained in order to prevent falls. See, also, Chapter 2.

Reasons given for restraining the elderly in hospitals or nursing homes

In hospitals and other community institutions, it is not uncommon for staff, who are afraid of litigation, to become over-protective and to prevent a confused person from walking by himself in order to lessen the risk of him falling, or to prevent him from invading other patient's space and causing them distress. Over-protection may lead to the use of physical restraints, such as cot-sides or sedatives and tranquillisers.

The law and the use of restraints

Save in certain circumstances, the use of physical restraints in the UK is not permitted. Clinical use of restraints raises moral and ethical dilemmas, particularly when an individual is too confused and is, therefore, not competent to make a decision himself.

While it is morally unjustifiable to restrain a person, there may be a justification for using restraints in the case of a person who, because of his agitation or tendency to wander, would require restriction for his own safety. The important point to note here is the safety of the individual, that is, it is being recommended for the person as being in his best interests and not for the interests of the staff. The law, under the Mental Health Act 1983, specifically permits such action in the circumstances described above. However, the Human Rights Act 1998, which became law in the UK in 2000, bestows a right not to be subjected to inhumane or degrading treatment; this could include the use of physical restraints.

Case 13: assessment of mental capacity to make a will

Facts of case

A solicitor asked a physician, who had been seeing the patient because of her memory difficulties, to see his client, in order to verify if she was able to make an informed decision concerning her legal affairs and, in particular, to confirm whether she had the capacity to make a will. The physician discussed the details of the client and, in particular, her assets with her solicitor and saw the patient in the presence of her solicitor.

Expert opinion

The physician assessed her mental state, including her short term memory and questioned her about her assets, asking to whom she wished to leave her money and property. The assessment revealed that:

- she had a very poor short term memory, could not name her friend, to whom she wanted to leave her house, and could not remember the physician's name even after she had been told it on two occasions a few minutes earlier;
- she did not have a true grasp of the extent of her assets, even after she had been reminded of them by the solicitor;
- she did not know where her friend lived and repeatedly gave her own address; and
- she did not appear to understand the difference between leaving the house in a will and transferring the house to her friend *inter vivos*.

Outcome

Based on his findings, the physician concluded that the patient lacked the sufficient mental capacity, probably as a result of her dementia, to make a will.

Case 14: the patient's family demanded the doctor change his mind on resuscitation status

Facts of case

An 88 year old lady was admitted with a large cerebral infarct (stroke). Prior to this, she was disabled as a result of long standing rheumatoid arthritis and required a considerable package of care from the community, as well as help from her husband and daughter. At the time of her admission, she was semi-comatose and, in addition, had a severe speech problem (receptive and expressive dysphasia), as well as a marked weakness of her left arm and left leg. The specialist registrar who saw her made a decision not to resuscitate her, in case of a cardio-respiratory arrest, on the grounds that: (a) it would not be successful; (b) she had a poor quality of life prior to admission; and (c) this decision would be in the best interests of the patient. The doctor informed the family of his decision.

Allegations made by the family

The patient's husband and daughter objected to this decision and demanded that she should be resuscitated in the event of a cardio-respiratory arrest and threatened to take legal advice and action, against both the hospital and the doctor.

Expert opinion

The consultant in charge of the medical care of the patient arranged to meet the patient's family and explained to them that, even if they did try to resuscitate her, they were not likely to succeed and that this DNR decision did not mean that their relative would be deprived of other medical treatments.

Outcome

The family accepted the consultant's explanation.

Comments

This case did not reach a solicitor. However, it highlights three important points:

(a) relatives and, on occasion, nursing staff falsely assume that a DNR order implies no treatment. On the contrary, patients who are not designated to be resuscitated receive antibiotics for infection and are given fluids and food as required;

(b) although relatives have a right to be involved in the decision making process, their views cannot override a clinical decision that is based on the best interests of the patient;

(c) the doctor's primary duty is to the patient and, in the case of a patient who is mentally incompetent, the doctor bases his decision on the course of action which would be of the greatest benefit to the patient.

CHAPTER 9

COMMON RISKS TO WHICH ELDERLY PATIENTS ARE ESPECIALLY VULNERABLE

INTRODUCTION

Because of the presence of normal ageing changes, often in conjunction with disease (which may itself be occult), elderly people are vulnerable to fall foul of common and simple hazards. Put in biological terms, they do not have the flexibility, adaptability or reserve capacity to maintain their equilibrium when challenged by a hostile environment and unexpected events.

POTENTIAL PROBLEMS

(a) Drugs.

(b) Trauma.

(c) Extremes of temperature.

(d) Fluid regulation.

(e) Driving and other traffic problems.

(f) Minor infections.

Drugs

See Chapter 10.

Trauma

See Chapters 2 and 7. Generally, there is a reduction in the ability to recover from trauma with increasing age. The number of elderly patients who are able to return to their premorbid state following an operation for a fractured neck of the femur is very disappointing.

Burns victims are known to recover in proportion to the severity of damage (the depth and area of the burn). However, in elderly patients, there is the added complication of their age, which has a severe detrimental effect. Death is much more likely to occur from a lesser extent of damage in the elderly than in fit, young patients.

Extremes of temperature

Cold

If exposed to severe cold for a long enough period of time, anybody will perish; for example, injured young mountaineers or fit seamen who fall into the icy North Sea may die of hypothermia. However, the problem is very much conceived as one exclusively affecting the old. The elderly are more vulnerable because of their inability to compensate (fight back) when exposed to the cold. In addition, as their temperature drops, they are more likely to experience problems in other areas due to impaired efficiency in other systems, for example, cardiac dysrhythmias. The insult (the temperature fall) does not need to be so severe or so prolonged as that needing to cause problems in fit, young people.

There is an association between environmental temperature and illness. It is because of this that the UK has an excess winter mortality. Our record in the UK is poor, much worse than some other countries with greater extremes of weather. The increased winter death rate in this country may be a reflection of our housing standards and the relative poverty of UK pensioners. Strokes, heart attacks, chest infections and falls all have a higher incidence in colder weather, hence, the winter bed crisis feared by all politicians and NHS managers!

Hypothermia accounts for less than 1% of the increased winter mortality – strokes and heart attacks account for 50%.

Hypothermia

This is defined as a body temperature of less than 35°C. As the usual clinical thermometer does not record below 35°C, the diagnosis can only be confirmed by using a special low reading instrument. This needs to be placed internally – usually rectally – as the often open mouth will again lead to false readings. Clinically, the patient will be puffy and cold to the touch; their pulse will be slow and their blood pressure will be low. If the diagnosis is suspected, then confirmation with a low reading thermometer is essential.

The facts

- Definition of hypothermia: core body temperature of less than 35°C.
- Patients become confused and drowsy when their body temperature falls below 32°C.
- Hypothermia causes 100 registered deaths in the UK per annum.
- Hypothermia accounts for 0.68% of hospital admissions, that is, 9,000 per annum in the UK.
- There is a 33% death rate if the core body temperature is between 30 and 35°C.

- There is a 70% death rate if the core body temperature is between 25 and 30°C.
- There is a 100% death rate if the core body temperature is less than 25°C.

Why elderly people fail to maintain a normal temperature

The main reason for this is the inadequate compensatory mechanisms in the elderly. The first step in protecting oneself from freezing is to be aware of a falling environmental temperature. Some elderly people are unable to do this, especially those with damage to their autonomic nervous system, such as diabetics and those who are heavily sedated, for example, with alcohol or phenothiazines. Normally, as we notice the temperature falling, protective actions are taken, for example, extra clothing is applied, windows are closed and the heating is turned up.

The next protective mechanism is for the body to conserve heat. This is achieved by restricting the peripheral circulation so that heat is not dissipated from the extremities. Patients with peripheral vascular disease, particularly diabetics, are disadvantaged in this ability.

If the situation worsens, the body will try to generate extra heat by muscle action, that is, shivering. Again, this ability is often impaired in elderly subjects, especially those with underlying diseases.

All of the above are internal responses to external changes. However, some elderly patients suffer a dramatic fall in body temperature due to internal problems alone. These problems are often of a vascular nature, such as a stroke or heart attack. It is assumed that the massive insult impairs autonomic temperature control – sometimes the patient's temperature rises and sometimes it falls. In either case, it is an indication of poor prognosis. The high death rate from hypothermia in old age is because it is the underlying pathology which is at fault, rather than the compensating mechanisms. Elderly patients may be found to be hypothermic when the environmental temperature is optimal, such as in a bed in a warm hospital ward.

Treatment of hypothermic patients

Treatment depends on the severity of the situation. If the patient's temperature is low, but their clinical condition is stable, that is, they are conscious and have a well maintained blood pressure and pulse, then simply providing warm clothing and hot drinks will be sufficient. An example would be a patient found lying on the ground in winter after just a brief period of exposure to the cold.

At the other extreme – an unconscious patient with poor vital signs – admission to hospital, preferably to an intensive care unit or a high dependency unit, would be required. An assessment of the patient will be needed to document any associated problems, but this can be difficult, as the patient cannot be exposed to examination for a long time or spend time on a trolley awaiting x-rays. The first task must be to prevent further loss of body heat by the provision of a heat retaining space blanket and by nursing the patient in a warm environment. Active re-warming should not be employed. Generally, the slower the return to a normal temperature, the better. If re-warming is too fast, the patient's circulation may be compromised; for example, the blood pressure may fall. Young, fit patients can be actively re-warmed, but not frail, elderly people.

Associated problems may need attention. For instance, the patient may be dehydrated, have a chest infection or have an electrolyte imbalance; all of these problems will require attention. The value of hormone replacements, especially hydrocortisone and thyroxine, is debatable, but is probably not required. Hydrocortisone, if given, is administered intravenously and should not endanger the patient. If thyroxine is given, it should be in the form of T3, which has a short half life and rapid action.

Who is at risk of hypothermia?

Those most at risk of contracting hypothermia are, essentially, the thin and frail, especially those with dementia, who may wander into hazardous conditions with inadequate protection. Their risks are increased if they are also on medication which may impair their ability to maintain a normal temperature. Phenothiazines are the greatest offenders; they were once used to precipitate hypothermia, in order to allow pioneer cardiac surgeons to operate!

Alcohol is another drug which is often involved. In excess, it often plays a role in the death of younger people who die of exposure, by causing dilatation of the blood vessels and thus increasing heat loss through the skin.

Any sedative taken in excess and leading to unconsciousness may expose the recipient to hypothermia if they are in a hostile environment.

Patients with poor circulatory reflexes are also at risk, especially diabetic patients with widespread atherosclerosis. Patients with extensive skin disease may also be unable to conserve their body heat and may even lose extra heat through their skin because of its increased vascularity.

Any patient who has experienced one episode of hypothermia is at increased risk of further recurrences. In such circumstances, extra precautions should be taken to avoid potentially dangerous situations.

Heat

This is not a great problem in this country for obvious reasons! However, when a prolonged heatwave does occur, the mortality rate in older people rises. The mechanism of death is usually through strokes and myocardial infarction. Frail, elderly people are at a greater risk of becoming dehydrated, often because of their reluctance to drink large amounts of fluid. Their thirst mechanism, like their temperature control mechanism, may be blunted. The resulting dehydration (which may be complicated by salt deficiency) will expose them to the risk of thrombotic episodes and possibly dysrhythmias. Their concurrent underlying medical problems and their prescribed medications may further complicate the situation.

Efforts should be made to keep elderly patients in a pleasant, ambient temperature during hot spells. This is not always appreciated by their carers and many of our institutions are more adept at retaining heat, rather than allowing for the circulation of cool air and heat dissipation. If the threat of global warming is delivered, then this will have to change.

Fluid regulation

This is clearly part of the problem in trying to maintain an equilibrium in hot weather. Another moment at which elderly patients are vulnerable to fluid and electrolyte changes is in the post-operative period.

Oral fluids may be actively restricted or may be impractical, because of nausea and vomiting. In addition, excess fluid and salts may be lost through surgical drains. The temptation for inexperienced junior doctors is to simply replace the fluid loss by the intravenous administration of dextrose saline – a very weak salt solution. The consequences may be 'flooding' and the precipitation of heart failure in those with impaired cardiac function. Furthermore, the blood salt levels may become depressed (hyponatraemia), with the result of confusion, cerebral swelling or even death in about 20% of cases. Patients who are on regular treatment with diuretics are particularly at risk and orthopaedic departments have a poor reputation for exposing their patients to these particular iatrogenic problems. These problems are avoidable.

In general, older people have a reduced sense of thirst; therefore, it is important that fluid intake is encouraged in times of increased need.

Driving and other traffic problems

In the UK, a normal driving licence is valid until the age of 70 years. After that age, the driver must renew their licence every three years and make a declaration of good health. The medical reasons why driving is prohibited are not age specific. However, as always, potential problems are more likely with increasing age. An essential prerequisite is good eyesight (with glasses if necessary), that is, being able to read a number plate at 25 yards and having full fields of vision; about one-third of elderly people have impaired visual acuity. Unpredictable episodes of loss of consciousness, whatever the cause (for example, epilepsy or dysrhythmias), also rule out driving.

More peripheral disabilities, such as arthritis, hemiparesis and amputation, will make driving more difficult, but will not always make it impossible or unsafe. In these circumstances, modifying the vehicle and a submission to undergo a further driving test may clarify the situation and allow a patient to remain 'at the wheel'.

Elderly people who drive become increasingly dependent on their vehicles as they become more frail. To have to give up driving is a great blow to self-respect and the maintenance of independence (especially in rural areas). However, there is often a temptation to continue driving when it is no longer safe. The driver may deny all difficulties – this is especially so in patients with dementia, who may lack all insight into their difficulties and the risks they run. The problem may be more apparent to the patient's friends and family, who always refuse to be passengers in the car.

Elderly drivers with dementia are a special case. They will have no insight into their own problems. In familiar circumstances and in a familiar car, they may remain good and competent drivers. However, in awkward situations and at times of crisis, they may be unable to cope and, therefore, should not be allowed to continue driving.

Figure 9.1   **The older car driver – accident involvement rates per million kilometres (1986, UK) (from Parliamentary Advisory Committee for Transport and Safety (PACTS), 1992)**

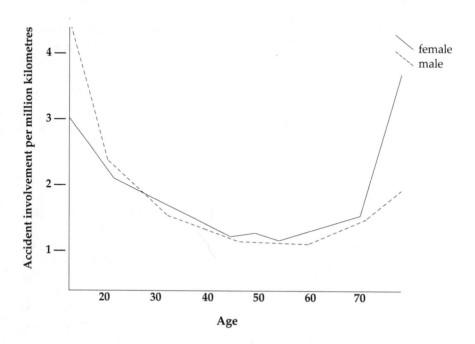

Figure 9.2   The older pedestrian – adult pedestrian casualties per million kilometres walked (from PACTS, 1992)

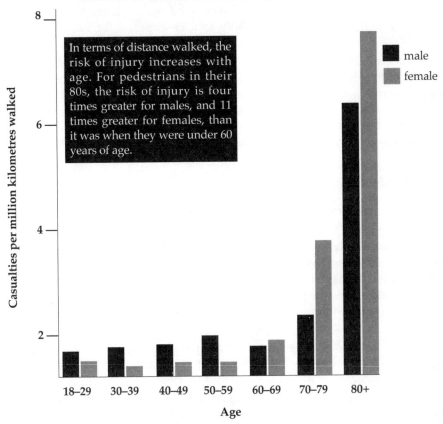

In terms of distance walked, the risk of injury increases with age. For pedestrians in their 80s, the risk of injury is four times greater for males, and 11 times greater for females, than it was when they were under 60 years of age.

Figure 9.3   Who is at risk – casualties aged 60 and over (1986, UK) (from PACTS, 1992)

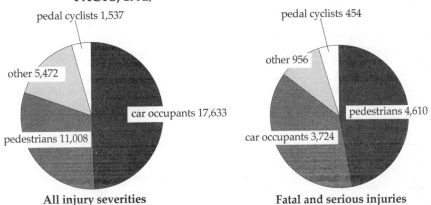

All injury severities   Fatal and serious injuries

All elderly patients who fear any change in their functional status should be advised to inform the DVLA and their insurance company. The number of elderly drivers is increasing and will continue to do so. Doctors must always inquire about driving and be willing to give appropriate advice for their elderly patients.

Unfortunately, the disabilities which impair driving – problems with vision, diminishing concentration, slow response and inability to judge speed and distance – also expose elderly pedestrians to accidents. If injury does occur, the elderly casualty is at greater risk of making a poor recovery than younger, fitter victims. Death on the roads is likely to become a bigger problem in geriatric medicine in future years.

Minor infections

What are considered as minor infections in the young may become major disasters in frail, elderly people.

Any patient already compromised by long standing chronic illness, poor nutrition and some medications (especially steroids) is much more likely to fall foul of a 'flu-like' illness or, in fact, influenza itself. It will not be the viral infection itself which is potentially fatal, but the secondary bacterial infection of the respiratory system which usually follows.

For the above reasons, the chief medical officer advises all elderly people to gain protection through the flu vaccination programme. Residents in institutions are perhaps even better protected if the staff are vaccinated, thus preventing infection being introduced into the home.

Pneumococcal vaccine is also available to protect vulnerable people. Those with chronic chest problems and a compromised immune system are eligible.

Almost every food poisoning outbreak demonstrates the vulnerability of frail, elderly people, who are often over-represented in the infected cases and the number of fatalities, an example being the E-coli outbreak in Scotland. This is because of the patient's inability to sustain the loss of fluids in diarrhoea and vomiting and thus to maintain an adequate circulation. Adequate, accurate and appropriate intravenous fluid and electrolyte replacement will be indicated at an earlier stage in elderly patients than in the young.

Special care in food hygiene is essential in all establishments where frail, elderly people live and it is part of the inspection and registration procedure for all care homes.

CHAPTER 10

TREATMENT IN THE ELDERLY

INTRODUCTION

The older a person becomes, the more likely they are to be on regular medication. This is simply because illness becomes increasingly common with increasing age. The elderly are perhaps the greatest beneficiaries from modern pharmacology.

Unfortunately, any drug capable of beneficial effects will also have the potential to cause harm. Modern drugs are double edged weapons, although much more preferable to the blunt or ineffective weapons of the past. The elderly are, therefore, also the group which suffers most from the ill effects of prescribed treatment.

Essentially, there are four reasons why elderly patients suffer from adverse drug reactions:

(a) the nature of the research base for the particular drug;

(b) ageing changes, affecting how the body handles drugs;

(c) multiple illnesses, which may also interfere with drug metabolism;

(d) interaction between several drugs taken together.

THE RESEARCH BASE

Most drug research is initially performed on healthy volunteers who are usually also young. The next stage in drug development is to give the preparation to a patient with a single disease. It is therefore hardly surprising that, when the same drug is given to a frail, elderly patient, it may not behave exactly as anticipated.

Slowly, there is an increasing awareness that new drugs need to be tested in the sort of 'real patients' who need them, that is, older, frailer subjects with multiple health problems.

AGEING CHANGES

Even healthy old people have some impairment in function in most of their organs. The gradual reduction in liver and kidney function which accompanies normal ageing will have an influence on how a person handles a drug. Many drugs need to be broken down in the liver, either before they can be effective or as part of the normal elimination process after they have served their purpose. Most drugs or their breakdown products are excreted out of the body through the kidneys.

Another mechanism is that of increased sensitivity of the target organ with increased age, for example, the ageing brain and some sedatives, tranquillisers and hypnotics.

MULTIPLE ILLNESSES

The normal ageing changes described above may be compounded by pathological changes in the same organs and tissues. Organ function may, therefore, be hindered by both the ageing changes and impairment caused by a disease affecting the same organ.

INTERACTION BETWEEN DRUGS

Many elderly patients quite rightly worry that their multiple drugs may work against each other. They know that it is unwise to mix one's drinks and that cocktails may have surprising effects. Their concerns are well founded and, in addition, alcohol should always be considered as a drug for this and all other purposes.

Clearly, the more drugs taken together, the greater the risk. As a rule of thumb, any doctor prescribing more than six preparations to a single patient should stop and think. As with all generalisations, there are many exceptions, but, generally, to be taking more than six different drugs means that harm is more likely to be the outcome than benefit.

How drugs cause problems

Ineffectiveness

The most common reason why a drug fails to be effective is because the diagnosis is wrong. If that is excluded as a cause, then the next consideration needs to be patient compliance, that is, whether the patient is taking the drug in the correct dose and at an appropriate time. Most elderly patients in full command of their faculties are usually obsessively correct and follow medical instructions without fail. Those who have a degree of dementia or depression may find it impossible to be compliant.

Patients who have side effects from a drug and find the treatment worse than their disease will usually also cease to follow the instructions they have been given. This behaviour is sometimes labelled as intelligent non-compliance!

Competition between two drugs taken at the same time may result in the loser becoming partially or completely ineffective. An example is where iron is given orally to correct anaemia, but the patient is also taking antacids at the same time. These can combine in the gut and the iron becomes non-available.

Drugs with opposing actions may also partially cancel out each other. For instance, a patient's heart failure may be well controlled until an anti-inflammatory drug is added to the patient's regime. The latter may cause retention of excess fluid and thus swamp the diuretic effect of the patient's concurrent therapy. As a consequence, the patient's control of their heart failure worsens. Although modern drugs have a high success rate, it has to be realised that, sometimes, there are individual exceptions. For instance, a very small percentage of patients who are accurately diagnosed as having idiopathic Parkinson's disease, and are known to be fully compliant in their treatment, fail to respond as expected. In these circumstances, alternative approaches to therapeutic intervention need to be explored.

Adverse reactions

Unexpected and unwanted results from drug treatment may take six forms.

Allergic reactions

These occur where a patient has had previous exposure to the drug and has developed antibodies against it or a byproduct of the drug. The reactions may range from mild skin rashes to painful joints, wheezing or dramatic life threatening collapse (anaphylactic shock). Once an allergic reaction has occurred, the patient must avoid all future contact with that drug and any related products. For example, if aspirin makes a patient breathless and wheezy, then allied drugs, such as non-steroidal anti-inflammatories, should also be avoided.

Because of the potential danger of allergic reactions, patients should be routinely asked about allergies and case records should clearly indicate when such problems exist.

Examples of drugs which commonly cause reactions are antibiotics (especially penicillin) and aspirin. Most drugs (and sometimes substances used in the manufacture and colouring of tablets) may cause problems in particularly sensitive individuals. The most vulnerable patients are those with known allergic conditions, such as asthma, hay fever and eczema.

Overdosage

This may result from a straightforward prescribing error, for example, through ignorance or miscalculation, such as misplacing a decimal point or confusion over the units of measurement.

The common principle that 'one size fits all' is often inappropriate in elderly patients. Old people have a much greater variation in height, size, weight and metabolism than is found in the middle aged. What is therefore considered as a normal adult dose may be too much for a thin, frail, elderly lady.

Impaired metabolism (breakdown) of drugs may also lead to overdosage. The impairment may be due to ageing changes, illness or a combination of both. Kidney impairment is the most common example – in such a patient, a 'normal' dose of, for example, digoxin may be excessive.

Interactions

When drugs are taken together, they may compete to be absorbed, metabolised, transported around the body and excreted. As with all competitions, there will be winners and losers – the result will be that one drug may be more effective than anticipated and its rival less so. Potentially, the patient may experience an overdose of one of the drugs and a sub-optimal effect of the other. Either distortion may be potentially unpleasant or dangerous.

A fairly common and potentially dangerous interaction is between warfarin (an anti-coagulant, which thins the blood) and other common drugs, such as antibiotics and painkillers. If the warfarin becomes more effective than expected, the patient will be at risk of bleeding. Alternatively, if the effect is that warfarin is reduced in effectiveness, a thrombosis may occur.

Side effects

Drug companies spend a lot of research time, effort and money on trying to produce 'selective drugs'. Their aim is to provide a drug with a single effect. Unfortunately, many drugs have additional effects aside from the main action for which it is given. If the drug is given for life saving purposes or the alleviation of severe symptoms, any side effect may be a price worth paying. The double effect of opiates in pain control in palliative care is perhaps the best known example; pain is relieved but, when large doses of opiates are used, respiration will be impaired and nausea, vomiting and constipation will be caused. The last three symptoms can be counteracted, but the associated respiratory suppression may accelerate death.

When a drug is used for fairly minor problems, the patient should not and probably would not tolerate having their well being impaired by inconvenient side effects. Whether the treatment is worthwhile or not is probably best judged by the patient who is well informed of the reasons for treatment and the consequences of not being treated. The patient will then be best placed to make the 'quality of life' decision which has to be made against potential benefits and risks.

Common unwanted side effects are headaches, dizziness, drowsiness, indigestion, constipation and nausea. Most are not potentially dangerous, but they can seriously impair the enjoyment of life. Some can have serious consequences, for example, drowsiness if the patient is driving or dizziness if it is due to a drop in blood pressure (postural hypotension) on standing, which may precipitate a serious fall. The correct course to take is a matter of judgment and one best made in consultation between patient and doctor.

Precipitation of other diseases

It is well known that drugs can cause disease – iatrogenic diseases. It is estimated that about 15% of admissions of elderly patients to hospital are caused by the consequences of their drug treatment. Diuretics (water tablets), given for heart failure, may bring to light previously occult diabetes mellitus in a susceptible patient. The same diuretics may cause gout in another patient. Powerful tranquillisers may cause stiffness and rigidity, similar to that seen in Parkinson's disease. Anti-inflammatory drugs, given for arthritis, may cause heart failure or renal failure in a vulnerable patient. Elderly patients are more likely than most to be disadvantaged by their treatment in this way.

Drugs which are withdrawn

This may occur inadvertently or a drug may be intentionally withdrawn, but too rapidly. Patients who are addicted to night sedation or alcohol may not report their habits on admission to hospital and unexpected episodes of disturbed behaviour may then occur when the patient ceases to follow their normal habit.

When some drugs are withdrawn too rapidly, a rebound phenomenon may occur. Examples are the stopping of beta-blockers, which may precipitate an episode of angina. Sudden withdrawal of warfarin may result in a thrombotic episode.

Other drug related problems in old age

Cost

New drugs are usually expensive and, if designed for common conditions, can potentially outstrip available budgets. An example is the new preparations for Alzheimer's disease, which have had their use severely restricted by some health authorities – known as 'postcode rationing'. In the future, such decisions are likely to be made nationally, by organisations such as the National Institute for Clinical Excellence (NICE). See Chapter 18 for further discussion on rationing.

Lifestyle drugs

Are patients entitled to free treatment for non-serious, non-life threatening conditions, for example, baldness, impotence or dissatisfaction with the shape of their nose? With restricted NHS resources, such problems should be the individual's responsibility and at their own cost.

Self-prescribing

This has been much encouraged by the Government, but it should not be overlooked that medicines bought without prescription may interreact with prescribed drugs. Many patients fail to recognise that their 'over the counter drugs' are, in fact, medicines and should be mentioned to their doctor when they are seeking additional treatment. Herbal remedies and alcohol should also be declared and not concealed. For various reasons, patients may be reluctant to be open about such habits.

Some elderly patients may assume that the lifelong use of laxatives may not be worthy of mention to their doctor. Such preparations become old friends and are not considered by the patient to be medicines.

Consumer resistance

This is allowed and should be respected, so long as the doctor has fully informed the patient of the consequences of not following his advice. The episode should be well documented in the patient's records.

Unrealistic expectations

There are many wonderful modern drugs, but they rarely cure; usually, they only modify disease behaviour. Chronic degenerative diseases, such as Parkinson's disease, continue to progress in spite of treatment. Chronic recurrent diseases, for example, depression, may recur once a course of therapy has been completed. Bacteria can become resistant to antibiotics. Modern medicines have been successful in prolonging life, but all lives still come to an end.

GUIDELINES FOR GOOD PRACTICE

The following points are suggestions for good practice to ensure safe and effective medical treatment in frail, elderly patients with complex needs and problems:

- make a diagnosis – in fact, the patient is likely to have several;
- list the diagnoses in priority order, in consultation with the patient where possible;

- decide which must be treated – some may have to be set aside, because the treatment of one disease may aggravate another;
- use established, familiar and trusted drugs, and check on allergies;
- use the minimum number of drugs – generally, start with a low dose and increase slowly until effective or toxic ('start low, go slow');
- if a drug is added or removed from the regime, stop and think about interreactions;
- regularly review medications taken – none should be continued if their usage is no longer justified;
- simplify drug regimes to assist patient compliance, for example, wherever possible, use once daily doses;
- listen to the patient's views and description of symptoms, as well as their fears about adverse effects.

THE LONG TERM EFFECTS OF SURGICAL TREATMENT

A successful surgical procedure may be complicated by long term adverse effects, which may occur many years after the initial operation. Three examples are given:

- post-gastrectomy – as a consequence of structural changes, the patient may suffer from malabsorption of vitamin B12 and vitamin D, leading to serious and severe forms of anaemia and disabling bone disease (osteomalacia). Post-gastrectomy patients should be monitored for this problem or at least warned and asked to report any relevant symptoms. The same complications can occur in any patient who has been left with a stricture or blind loop after bowel surgery;
- post-thyroidectomy myxoedema – patients who have part of their thyroid gland removed because of its overactivity may eventually swing to the other extreme. The change is slow and silent and, if not actively sought, may be overlooked for years;
- post-intra-cranial surgery epilepsy – many neurosurgeons routinely prescribe post-operative anti-convulsants to patients who have undergone intra-cranial surgery, in order to try to avoid this long term complication.

DRUG TAKING IN THE ELDERLY – SOME FACTS

- Hypnotics are taken by 16% of elderly people.
- Sixty per cent of elderly people take regular medication.
- Twenty per cent of elderly patients are taking three or more preparations.

- One-third of medications are for diseases of the cardiovascular system.
- Forty per cent of patients over the age of 80 are taking diuretics.
- One-third of prescribed drugs are taken for more than five years.
- Three-quarters of prescribed drugs are taken for more than one year.
- Patients over 70 years are seven times more likely to have an adverse drug reaction than patients under 30.
- Fifteen per cent of hospital admissions are related to drug treatment.
- Almost 8% of elderly people drink alcohol to excess.
- Two per cent of hospital admissions of elderly people are related to alcohol abuse.

Case 15: fit, elderly lady – overdosage of diazepam

Facts of case

A fit 88 year old lady, who was personally independent and an active carer for her grandson, who had learning difficulties, developed dyspeptic symptoms. She was seen in an out-patient clinic and was later admitted to a private hospital for an endoscopy. This was to be as a day case.

She was given intravenous diazepam as pre-medication. The dose given was 20 mg (the normal dose for 'an adult'). However, it is a drug which should be used cautiously in old patients, especially those who are physically small. The patient's weight was only 40 kg. The makers of the drug recommend an intravenous dose of between 0.1 and 0.2 mg per kilogram body weight, that is, a maximum of 8 mg for a lady of her weight.

The patient made a poor recovery from the procedure and had to stay in hospital overnight. On being taken home, she was still drowsy, could not walk and needed help with feeding. She was later admitted to another hospital, where evidence of peritonitis was found, as well as possible lateralising signs in her central nervous system.

Although she improved, she was never again able to assist in the care of her grandson and did herself require help with activities of daily living.

The claimant argued that the overdosage of diazepam exposed her to the risk of gastro-duodenal perforation and brain damage. This was denied by the defence, who claimed that she had received as much sedation as she needed.

Outcome

However, the case was later settled out of court for a large, undisclosed sum.

SURGERY IN ELDERLY PATIENTS

All patients should be aware that there are risks attached to all forms of surgical intervention. Usually, the risks are low and worth taking. Unfortunately, the risks rise with increasing age, but the benefits can still be enormous. Much skill and experience is needed from all those involved in the surgical care of elderly patients – their nurses, anaesthetists, surgeons and therapists.

The recent national confidential enquiry into peri-operative deaths 'at the extremes of age' has highlighted many problems relating to the increased mortality of very elderly patients within surgical departments. The report recommends that emergencies in old age should be dealt with promptly (within 24 hours), with the most experienced staff undertaking the work. It is often a very fine balance as to how much time can be devoted to improving the general condition of a very sick, elderly patient before embarking on an operation.

It should also be appreciated that, just because a procedure is possible, it is not always advisable or desirable. Mentally competent patients will be able to make this difficult decision for themselves once the situation has been explained to them. Some will have indicated in advance (by a living will or an advance directive) their wishes in these matters. In many other cases, the difficult choices will have to be made by others in the best interests of the patient. In these situations, experienced practitioners, assisted by the patient's family and friends, are most likely to make the correct decision.

Surgery should only be embarked upon when the following criteria have been satisfied:

- are the expectations achievable and realistic?;
- has the patient's co-morbidity problems been treated to an optimal level?;
- does the patient understand what will be expected of them?;
- is the anaesthetist confident about the degree of control that they have over the situation?; and
- will the patient be able to participate in an active rehabilitation programme in the post-operative period?

If there is an undue delay in operating, or if surgery is performed on a poorly prepared patient, then the risks of disaster will be high. The patient may not succumb to the presenting condition, but the consequent collapse of other systems may directly cause death. Death from a myocardial infarction or a stroke are particular risks for frail patients suffering from poor circulation, which can then be further compromised by blood and fluid loss, hypotension or hypoxia (oxygen starvation).

CHAPTER 11

VASCULAR DISEASE

INTRODUCTION

When all forms of vascular disease (strokes, heart attacks, heart failure and peripheral vascular disease) are combined, they will be seen to be responsible for the majority of deaths within the UK. It is only when heart disease and strokes are separated that malignant disease (cancer) is allowed to slip into second place, behind heart disease and ahead of strokes.

The head and the heart have much in common, especially in their responses to vascular disease (that is, the effect on their blood supply). Essentially, vascular disease can take two forms – the narrowing of the vessels with a reduction in the vessel lumen, thus leading to impaired blood supply (ischaemia), or vessel rupture, causing haemorrhage and resulting in tissue damage and/or death (necrosis).

HEART DISEASE

This is the commonest cause of death in the UK. It may be responsible through slow, progressive heart failure or suddenly, after an acute heart attack. The two are not mutually exclusive and recurrent heart attacks may result in death through chronic heart failure.

Heart failure

The main clinical features are breathlessness, reduced effort tolerance (tiredness and fatigue) and fluid retention, especially presenting as ankle swelling or sudden breathlessness. All of these symptoms can, of course, have alternative explanations.

A heart may fail because it has become inefficient, usually because one or more of its valves becomes leaky or too tight. It may also fail because it is overworked, that is, pumping against an increased blood pressure. It may fail because it is under-nourished, that is, its own blood supply is inadequate. This is known as myocardial ischaemia and classically presents as angina (that is, a heart crying for help when under pressure). This is, of course, a gross over-simplification. The mechanisms can occur together and each may have many obscure causes.

Elderly patients may be disadvantaged because many of their symptoms may be inaccurately put down to old age, such as shortness of breath and tiredness. Patients may thus be denied appropriate treatment which could help them. Some symptoms or signs might be misinterpreted and inappropriate treatment given, such as asthma treatment for their breathlessness. Under-treatment will be a potential consequence of these pitfalls.

Over-treatment is also a potential problem. Over-enthusiastic treatment with diuretics (water tablets) may cause the patient to become dehydrated. Making the assumption that the patient's swollen ankles is due to heart failure, when it is, in fact, due to renal failure, may also expose the patient to inappropriate treatment.

Clearly, the treatment of heart failure in old age is very much a matter of judgment and balance. To err too much in either direction can result in great cost to the patient. For a general discussion on the complications of medical treatment in elderly patients, see Chapter 10.

Heart attacks

When a middle aged lawyer falls to the ground, clutching his chest and complaining of severe tight chest pain, most onlookers would probably and correctly diagnose a heart attack (an acute myocardial infarction or a coronary thrombosis). Unfortunately, the older the victim, the more likely they are to present in a less spectacular and less obvious fashion. Not all heart attacks are accompanied by chest pain; indeed, sometimes, chest pain can be atypical. This is one reason why the diagnosis of an acute myocardial infarction may be delayed in an older person.

Normally, the first step to support the diagnosis of an acute myocardial infarction is to carry out an electrocardiogram (ECG) on arrival at hospital or when the ambulance arrives. Again, evidence provided by the ECG may be inconclusive or misleading in elderly people. If they have had a previous episode of this or long standing chronic myocardial ischaemia, then their tracing may be confusing. The next step in diagnosis is to check blood enzyme levels. These include transaminases from muscles, which are released when the muscles are damaged, as are heart muscle fibres in an acute myocardial infarction. However, if other muscles are damaged, for example, as the patient falls to the ground (for any reason), the muscles damaged in the fall will also release transaminases. It is possible to specifically measure those transaminases originating from the heart muscle, but all of this takes time.

Time is becoming increasingly important in the management of an acute myocardial infarction because of the availability of 'clot busting drugs', such as streptokinase, which can assist in the re-opening of a blocked coronary artery. The sooner such treatment is given, the better; after about six hours following an attack, little, if any, benefit will be gained by giving this treatment, which, in itself, also carries some risk of causing bleeding, especially in the brain.

Because elderly patients are at greater risk of dying than younger subjects with a myocardial infarction, they potentially have a greater opportunity for benefit (in spite of the risks of complications also being increased). The urgency and accuracy of diagnosis and intervention are, therefore, very important in elderly patients. However, they are more likely than most patients to suffer from delay, due to:

- atypical presentation;
- a lack of urgency on the part of the ambulance service;
- confusion over the diagnosis;
- anxieties about complications of treatment.

As a consequence, there is unfortunately good evidence that many elderly myocardial infarction patients are denied effective therapy.

Having survived a heart attack, there should be good evidence in the medical records that consideration has been given to the task of trying to prevent further episodes. Available treatments include regular, low doses of aspirin, ACE inhibitors, beta-blockers and statins. In many elderly patients, there will be strong contra-indications to using some of these medications, because of co-morbidity.

A period of rehabilitation will be needed by survivors and some will require further investigation to explore the possibility of other interventions for revascularisation. Elderly patients should not be excluded from these activities or procedures on the basis of age alone.

Cardiopulmonary resuscitation

Patients experiencing an acute myocardial infarction are prime candidates for cardiopulmonary collapse, due to disorganised electrical transmission in the heart, leading to irregular heart rhythms (dysrhythmias). Unfortunately, the success of techniques in these situations has been extrapolated to other serious life threatening episodes. This is not always justified or appropriate. Patients and relatives frequently have unrealistic expectations concerning attempts at resuscitation and are unaware of the distressing aspects of such activity when inappropriate. CPR decisions are not easy and each patient must be assessed individually from the facts available. However, it has to be accepted that it is not always appropriate to try resuscitation and the overall results (the number of successful discharges from hospital) are much lower than most people appreciate. However, once again, age alone should not be the main criterion on which such decisions are made.

STROKES

Pathophysiology

A stroke is a result of damage to the brain because of impairment of the blood supply to a particular area. It is common and, in an average health district in the UK with a population of about a quarter of a million, there will be one or two strokes daily. Most (75%) will be in patients of pensionable age – the older the subject, the greater the risk.

The nature of the vascular incident (cerebrovascular accident (CVA)) will be thrombotic in about 90% of cases. The thrombus may form locally; patients with viscous blood (those who are dehydrated or who have abnormal blood), those with abnormal (inflamed) arteries and those with narrowed arteries are all at the greatest risk. Sometimes, the initial problem is an embolus, that is, a small clot from elsewhere (usually from the heart or vessels supplying the brain – the carotid or vertebral arteries) which forms the basis of a progressive thrombosis. The remaining 10% of strokes will be due to bleeding – a cerebral haemorrhage. Groups at especially high risk are those with vascular malformations, for example, aneurysms (these are little berry-like protrusions on vessels on the surface of the brain which, on rupturing, cause a subarachnoid haemorrhage (SAH)). Patients with thin blood, for example, those on anti-coagulants, are also at greater risk.

Presentation

The onset of the stroke may be rapid and apoplectic; the rupture of a berry aneurysm is the best example. It may, alternatively, be slow and gradual or it may even be intermittent.

The extent of the stroke may range from unconsciousness, with total paralysis, to merely a slight weakness of a limb or perhaps difficulty with speech or vision.

The first medical responsibility is to protect life if the patient is unconscious and in danger of dying. The second responsibility is to confirm the diagnosis. About 5% of patients who appear to have suffered a stroke, that is, have a neurological deficit of sudden onset, will have non-vascular causes and are, therefore, not strokes. Such causes range from tumours to clots between the brain and the skull. This small group needs to be identified, as neurosurgical intervention may be curative.

Investigation

The best method of confirming the nature of the underlying pathology is the performance of a head CT scan. Such scans are now available in most district general hospitals (DGHs), although a 24 hour service is not always possible; even in centres with good resources, delays may occur because of the pressure of work. The scan should reveal those patients with a space occupying lesion (a clot or tumour). It should also be able to identify a recent cerebral haemorrhage, but a recent thrombosis may not be identifiable. However, from the point of immediate care, it is those bleeding or with tumours who are in greatest need of identification.

Management

Ideally, the next step would be one of damage limitation. Unfortunately, health professionals are not yet very good at this. The aim would be to allow or encourage healing of the area of brain which has been damaged by ischaemia, but is not yet dead. Many techniques of infusions and drugs have been used, but with no real demonstrated benefits (some have probably been harmful). The best that can be attempted at present is a maintenance of normality with regard to electrolyte and fluid balance and temperature control. Control of blood pressure is much more uncertain and is a debatable point. Hopefully, through the development of 'acute stroke units', success will be achieved in damage limitation in the near future.

There is a greater rate of success in protecting patients from further episodes of thrombosis. Regular low doses of aspirin are safe and effective. Selective drugs to reduce platelet stickiness (platelets are particles in the blood which play an active role in clotting) and the use of warfarin (an anti-coagulant) in embolic cases are known to be effective, so long as there are no strong contra-indications. Some practitioners will wait for a period of seven to 10 days following a stroke before starting warfarin, whilst others are more impatient. The long term control of high blood pressure (hypertension) and of pulse irregularities are accepted as being beneficial.

The remaining activity during the acute phase is to not forget about the rest of the patient. Many will have concurrent illnesses, such as diabetes, which will require good control; some will also suffer from heart failure. Stroke patients also need to be protected from the complications of their new disabilities; for example, swallowing may be impaired and the patient will thus be exposed to the risk of an aspiration pneumonia (due to food or fluids 'going down the wrong way'). Pressure areas will need protection and contractures setting up in paralysed limbs will need to be prevented by skilled nursing or physiotherapy.

A stroke is a lethal condition and about one-third of patients die, some because of the extent of the original insult, but more because of mismanagement or the development of complications. This is especially true in patients already disadvantaged by other chronic medical conditions.

As soon as possible, and certainly after the patient has stabilised, active rehabilitation should be commenced. This is a skilled intensive activity, requiring the input of an effective multi-disciplinary team, comprising of nurses, doctors, therapists, the patient and their family. Whether this service is best provided in a designated 'stroke unit' or by a dedicated, but peripatetic, team is debatable; generally, the former arrangement is gaining in support. Whichever method is used, it is essential that both the correct quality, quantity and diversity of staff is provided. The patient also needs to be both willing and able to participate. Co-morbidity may be a problem, as may the onset of depression. The latter will need to be identified and treated. Dementia is the most significant bar to rehabilitation; it does not make it impossible, but does make it much more difficult. A slower, more subtle form of rehabilitation is needed than is usually provided in 'active' rehabilitation settings.

Rehabilitation

A common complaint about rehabilitation is that the patient does not get enough time with the therapist. However, in efficiently run departments, every waking moment is part of the patient's treatment, as nurses, friends and helpers should be reinforcing the instructions of the therapist. Another difficult decision is the duration and termination of rehabilitation. The degree of recovery from a stroke is very variable, from total to non-existent. Generally, the greatest improvement will have been achieved within three months of the event, but there are exceptions. Regular reviews of stroke patients should therefore be maintained, in case there is a sudden and unexpected improvement at a later date, which can then be further encouraged with active interventions.

Transient ischaemic attacks (TIAs)

Transient ischaemic attacks (TIAs) are mini strokes, which come and go within 24 hours. They must also be associated with either lateralising signs (affecting the right or left side), speech or visual disturbances in order to qualify for this specific label. 'Funny turns' and so on should not be included. Most episodes are embolic. These attacks are important, as they often act as harbingers of true strokes. Likely sources of emboli are the heart (clots in chambers, on the heart wall or on valves) or the carotid circulation (arising from atheromatous plaques on the arterial walls). Where the patient is otherwise well, surgical removal of the plaque is indicated if there is also evidence of significant narrowing of the lumen. If the indications for surgery are not fulfilled, then protection with anti-coagulants or a reduction in platelet adhesiveness (using aspirin or similar drugs) may be appropriate, so long as there are no contra-indications to such treatment.

Patients with atrial fibrillation are particularly at risk. They have an irregularly irregular heart rate, with incomplete emptying of the first chamber of the heart. A clot may then form in the cavity of the chamber and showers of emboli may disperse into the circulation. If possible, these patients should be on warfarin and have their heart rate controlled (usually with digoxin). The decision is difficult in the very old. Those with compliance problems, those likely to fall frequently and patients who have need of frequent changes of their other medications are often unsuitable for such treatment. However, at the very least, there should be evidence that the possibility of warfarin treatment has been considered. Some suitable elderly patients may, of course, decline to accept the advice they are given – this should be accepted, but documented.

PERIPHERAL VASCULAR DISEASE

Pathophysiology

This is essentially poor circulation, usually affecting the legs. It can range from claudication, that is, calf pain on walking (relieved by rest – it is like angina in the chest), through to tissue death (gangrene), requiring amputation of the damaged limb. The underlying pathology is a narrowing of the arteries due to atheroma. It is particularly common in patients with diabetes and in heavy smokers. Some cases are due to inflammation of the arteries (arteritis); these may respond to treatment with steroids and other immuno-suppressives, as there is often an auto-immune element to the process.

Management

In early cases of ischaemia, it will hopefully be possible to demonstrate restricted blood flow by Doppler and arteriography. If a discrete stenosis (a narrowing) is found, it may be dilated by balloon techniques or bypassed surgically. Unfortunately, the underlying pathological changes are often widespread and temporary relief may be obtained by surgical intervention, only for the symptoms to recur later. Sympathectomy is a severing of the autonomic nervous system which supplies the affected limb. It may allow the narrowed arteries to dilate, but results are often disappointing.

If an amputation is carried out, severe phantom limb pain may be a residual problem. Treatment can be difficult, but anti-depressants can help, as can anti-convulsants. Post-operatively, amputees need an extensive rehabilitation programme. Many elderly patients will be too frail to manage with an artificial limb and the best that might be achieved in these circumstances is wheelchair independence.

When all else fails, the severe pain of limb ischaemia must be treated palliatively with appropriate doses of opiates (morphine related drugs).

Patients with peripheral limb ischaemia should not take beta-blockers for other conditions, such as to control angina or blood pressure. These drugs have an adverse affect on the peripheral circulation and can make a bad situation worse. It should also be realised that beta-blocker eye drops are also absorbed and can have an effect on the peripheral circulation.

LEG ULCERS

Ankle ulceration is most commonly due to poor venous return, especially in middle aged patients. The ulcers may become very large, infected and offensive. With effective cleaning and compression bandaging, they can be encouraged to heal, but the risk of recurrence is ever present.

In elderly patients, ankle ulcers may be arterial or a mixture of both venous and arterial impairment. Arterial ulcers are likely to be painful, especially when in bed at night. Management is more difficult, as tight bandaging should be avoided. If it is possible to improve the arterial circulation by surgical intervention, then the opportunity should be taken.

Large, clean ulcers can be effectively treated by skin grafting by plastic surgeons, but a reasonable underlying arterial circulation is required if healing is to be achieved.

An ankle ulcer may result from a very minor injury, but, when healing fails to occur, it will usually be due to the underlying circulatory problems.

HYPERTENSION (RAISED BLOOD PRESSURE)

Introduction

Blood pressure tends to rise with increasing age. About one-half of the population aged over 65 years can be considered to be hypertensive. The definition of hypertension has varied over the years. The recent British standard has been taken as 160/90 mm Hg. However, there is a growing desire to reduce the acceptable upper limits to 140/80 mm Hg. The upper figure is known as the systolic and was initially considered to be of less significance than the lower figure (the diastolic). This has recently been reversed. Elderly people are particularly likely to suffer from systolic hypertension.

The blood pressure varies considerably in any individual, depending on such factors as their activity or anxiety levels. A single blood pressure reading should not be relied upon before initiating treatment. At least three readings on three separate occasions must be taken. Some patients increase their blood pressure even at the prospect of having it measured (white coat hypertension). If there are doubts about the validity of blood pressure measurements, the solution is to carry out continuous monitoring whilst the patient leads their normal life. Unfortunately, this facility is not always available. There is accumulating evidence that sustained hypertension in elderly patients should be treated. Since elderly patients had previously been excluded from blood pressure trials, this information has been slow in being acquired and the position in the very old (those aged over 90) remains uncertain. If, on examination and investigation, the patient shows evidence of end organ damage, then the necessity for treatment is more compelling. The sort of damage that the professional should look out for is impaired kidney function, damage to the eyes and evidence of heart failure or previous strokes. Any patient who is also diabetic is particularly vulnerable to the ravages of hypertension.

Management

Once it has been decided that a reduction in blood pressure is needed, the next decision is the choice of drug management. All hypertensive patients should be encouraged to achieve an ideal weight, to reduce salt intake (in cooking), to take regular exercise and to avoid smoking. In mild cases, these measures, if successfully accomplished, may be sufficient to bring the blood pressure down to an acceptable level (usually 140/80 mm Hg or less).

When additional help is required, drugs will need to be prescribed. The traditional method is a step wise progression. First, the use of simple diuretics, usually bendrofluazide, is commenced. If this fails, then a beta-blocker (for example, atenolol) would be added, then, if necessary, a calcium channel blocker (for example, nifedipine) and, finally, an ACE inhibitor (for example, captopril).

Treatment in elderly patients is often complicated by contra-indications to some of the above drugs. Bendrofluazide can worsen the sugar control of diabetics and may precipitate gout in some susceptible patients. Beta-blockers are particularly dangerous in patients with heart failure, asthma or peripheral vascular disease. Calcium channel blockers may cause flushing and ankle swelling. ACE inhibitors may cause an irritating, dry cough. In addition, some elderly patients find the side effects from some of these drugs intolerable, especially the lethargy caused by beta-blockers.

Finding the right drug or combination of drugs for each individual patient is difficult. It is also important to avoid sudden and dramatic changes to the blood pressure in elderly patients who are likely to have an already compromised circulatory system. Postural hypotension (the blood pressure falling on standing up) is another unwelcome complication of many forms of blood pressure control. In frail, elderly patients, a fall in blood pressure on standing may precipitate a fall; the resulting trauma (for example, a fractured neck of the femur) may lead to the patient's death.

There are clearly difficulties in the treatment of raised blood pressure in old age. However, there are also considerable potential benefits, especially the protection from strokes, heart failure and other forms of end organ damage. There is also the potential to protect from myocardial infarction, although this is less dramatic and is supported by less well documented evidence.

CONCLUSION

As most of us are likely to die as a consequence of vascular disease, there is great scope to influence the natural progression of circulatory pathology. However, any intervention must be performed in a steady and reasoned fashion. Sudden, impulsive action and changes are to be discouraged; slow, measured progress is best. Vascular disease is a rapidly changing field. There is much pressure from the pharmaceutical industry and many academics to rush ahead. Fashion in this field may change year by year and not always in a logical way. A great deal of reflection and prudence is needed for the successful management of frail, elderly patients with vascular problems.

Demonstrating the co-morbidity of various forms of vascular disease

(Information gathered from 1,802 geriatric in-patients aged between 60 and 102 (mean age 80 years).)

- Of patients with coronary artery disease, 32% will also have evidence of an ischaemic stoke.

- Of patients with coronary artery disease, 26% will also have evidence of peripheral vascular disease.

- Of patients with an ischaemic stroke, 56% will also have evidence of coronary artery disease.

- Of patients with an ischaemic stroke, 28% will also have evidence of peripheral vascular disease.

- Of patients with peripheral vascular disease, 68% will also have evidence of coronary artery disease.

- Of patients with peripheral vascular disease, 82% will also have evidence of previous ischaemic stroke.

Reduction in serious consequences in older patients on treatment of hypertension

Cardiovascular events	Strokes	Coronary heart disease	All mortality
30–33%	35–40%	15–26%	16%

Demonstrating the reduction in morbidity in patients older than 80 years who were treated for hypertension

Cardiovascular events	Strokes	Heart failure
22%	34%	39%

Strokes – the facts

- About one-third of victims die within the first month.
- About one-third of survivors develop depression.
- Less than one-third of survivors return to their previous level of activity.
- Approximately one-quarter of survivors fail to achieve unassisted walking.
- Between 10 and 20% of survivors will require long term, high dependency care.
- The recurrence rate for strokes is about 10% per annum.

Coronary artery disease – the facts

- At post-mortem, 70% of examinations in patients over 70 years of age show evidence of coronary artery disease.
- Ten per cent of hearts at post-mortem in patients older than 65 years have evidence of a new or old myocardial infarction.
- Twenty to thirty per cent of people over the age of 65 have clinical evidence of ischaemic heart disease.
- Fifteen to thirty per cent of myocardial infarctions in old age are silent.
- Eighty per cent of all deaths due to myocardial infarction occur in patients older than 65 years.
- Sixty per cent of all deaths due to myocardial infarction occur in patients older than 75 years.

- The post-myocardial infarction one year mortality rate is 12% in patients aged 65–75 years.
- The post-myocardial infarction one year mortality rate is 17% in patients older than 75 years.

Case 16: the importance of the widespread nature of vascular disease

Facts of case

An 88 year old woman complained of pain in her right calf on walking. An arteriogram showed fairly widespread atheromatous changes, but with a discrete lesion that could be bypassed.

The operation appeared to go well but, whilst in the recovery room, the patient collapsed and developed a left sided weakness, affecting her arm and leg. She never recovered consciousness and died. A post-mortem confirmed a cerebral thrombosis and widespread atheroma in the cerebral circulation. The operation site was given a clean bill of health.

Allegations made by the family

The family claimed that the operation was mismanaged and had caused the patient's stroke. The defence argued that the patient's arterial disease was widespread and the stroke was not caused by the successful operation.

Outcome

The case was dropped.

Case 17: the 'silent presentation' of myocardial infarction

Facts of case

A 92 year old woman was taken to her local Accident and Emergency department suffering from chest pains. Her ECG and cardiac enzyme levels failed to show any evidence of myocardial infarction. She was told that her pain was an episode of her usual angina and she was discharged home.

Later the same day, she fell at home. Her husband could not get her up and called the ambulance service. They felt that she looked unwell and decided to return her to the Accident and Emergency department. As a simple fall, she was triaged into a low category group. Her condition appeared stable on arrival but, several hours later, she was found collapsed on her trolley. A fresh ECG showed the acute changes of an acute myocardial infarction. She continued to deteriorate and died within hours, in spite of attempts at treatment and resuscitation.

Allegations made by the family

The patient's husband argued that she died because she was neglected on the trolley. The trust argued that she was appropriately categorised in Accident and Emergency and her collapse could not have been foreseen.

In retrospect, it was likely that her myocardial infarction had occurred at the time of her fall at home, but was missed because of the lack of chest pain or any other symptoms. When her condition worsened, she was treated appropriately, but unsuccessfully.

Outcome

Her family accepted this information and dropped the case.

Case 18: the risk of further heart damage

Facts of case

Five days before Christmas, a woman in her 70s was admitted to hospital because of chest pain. A diagnosis of an acute myocardial infarction was made on the basis of ECG changes and enzyme changes. She was treated appropriately with thrombolysis but, on the day after admission, had further chest pain, with a further extension of her myocardial infarction. There was a further complication of her management by the development of a pericardial friction rub. Again, appropriate medical management was instituted by the team managing her care. The patient was also known to be diabetic and, after some initial adjustment to her treatment, her diabetes again came under good control.

Seven days after admission to hospital, the patient was no longer in any pain and was mobile within the ward; she was very keen to return home. This was two days after Christmas and it was impossible to arrange any support for the patient at home, but the family were happy to return her to her own accommodation and provided transportation.

On the following day, the patient complained of being generally unwell and of shortness of breath. Her GP made some minor adjustments to her medication.

Since there was no improvement on the following day, the patient was admitted to hospital and died on the same day. A post-mortem confirmed that she had suffered a further myocardial infarction.

Allegations made by the family

The patient's family claimed that the patient had been discharged from hospital prematurely. The family felt that a hospital stay of 14 days was the minimum. It was explained that a seven day stay was fairly standard for someone having suffered a myocardial infarction; a discharge home at that time, in someone who was not in any pain and was mobile, was not inappropriate. There was also evidence in the nursing notes that the patient had received some counselling and advice regarding activities in her post-infarct period. The discharge had also been made at the patient's request and the family had participated by providing the transport home. It had been explained to the family that it would not be possible to arrange additional support because of the Christmas holiday period.

Outcome

The patient's family reluctantly accepted the explanation given and that a discharge after a seven day period was not inappropriate, in view of the patient's satisfactory progress as an in-patient. The fact that another myocardial infarction occurred was totally unpredictable and was in no way related to the way that her treatment had been managed.

CHAPTER 12

CANCER IN OLD AGE

GENERAL PRINCIPLES

Introduction

It is at the extremes of life that cancer strikes. In childhood, it occurs mainly in the form of blood disorders, such as acute leukaemia and cerebral tumours. Both of these conditions can occur in later life, but cancers of other organs and systems also become much more likely. After middle age, the incidence of cancer rises, but different forms peak at different ages. For example, lung cancer peaks relatively early, at about 65 years, but most others peak at about 80 years of age. There is some evidence of a tailing off in the very extremes of old age; this is supported by both clinical and post-mortem evidence. Patterns of cancers differ between the sexes, sometimes for obvious reasons; for example, prostatic cancer occurs only in men and gynaecological cancer occurs only in women. The other malignancy which shows a marked sex difference is breast cancer, which can affect both sexes, but is predominant in women, whereas most other malignancies tend to be more common in men.

An elderly person with cancer is also likely to have co-existent pathologies (co-morbidity). This concurrent progression of illnesses will complicate the presentation and management of the cancer. Cancer is the second most frequent form of death in those aged over 65. It is exceeded by heart disease and just outnumbers deaths from strokes. Most people who die of cancer are old.

Frequently, inappropriate assumptions are made with regard to cancer in old age, for example, it is less aggressive, less important and more readily accepted by the patient. However, cancers differ, patients differ and so do their doctors. It is essential that, in all cases, irrespective of age, a full assessment of the patient and their problems is made, all options are considered and a reasoned conclusion and management plan are decided upon; the patient, as always, having the casting vote.

Unfortunately, many of the questions relating to malignant disease and its treatment in old age remain unanswered. This is because patients of advanced years are often excluded from the clinical trials. As elderly patients demand to be taken seriously, this will be corrected, and rightly so, for the elderly are at the greatest risk.

Figure 12.1   **Incidence of cancer as related to increasing age (all malignant neoplasms excluding melanoma skin) (from the East Anglian Cancer Registry and Intelligence Units, Cambridge, 1997)**

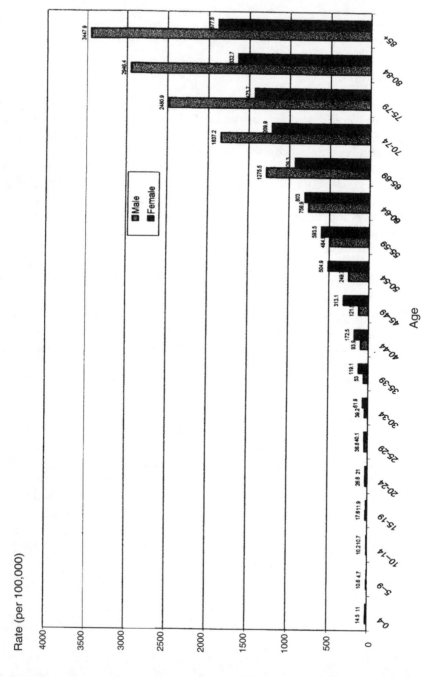

Screening

This allows the early detection of a condition before symptoms and signs are apparent. The requirements of a screening programme are as follows:

(a) the condition should be common;

(b) the condition must have serious consequences;

(c) the screening technique must be simple and safe;

(d) the screening technique must be efficient, that is, with few false positives or false negatives;

(e) the treatment must be cost effective.

Current examples are:

(a) breast cancer – established, but age restricted;

(b) cervical cancer;

(c) colorectal cancer – being piloted; and

(d) cancer of the prostate – needing more information.

Screening does not obviate the need for health education. Elderly people should be provided with the necessary information to enable them to detect early changes that may indicate the possibility of an underlying cancer. For example, elderly women should be encouraged to continue to self-examine their breasts throughout life.

Figure 12.2   **Age related incidence of cancer in men and women (from Yancik, R and Ries, LA, 'Cancer in older persons. Magnitude of the problem: how do we apply what we know?' (1994) Cancer 74: 1995–2003)**

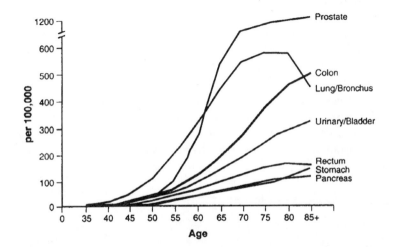

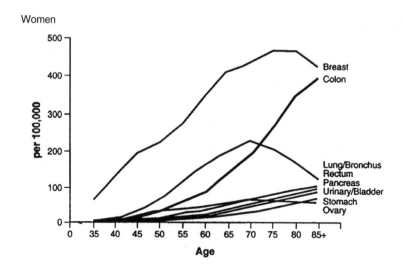

Reasons for delayed diagnosis in elderly patients

(a) Stoicism on the part of the patient.

(b) The doctor and/or patient who takes the view that 'it's your age'.

(c) The doctor and/or patient who takes the view that 'it's your old problem'.

(d) A failure to take elderly patients seriously.

(e) A difficulty in performing investigations.

Age related difficulties in diagnosis

Many cancers are slow growing and develop silently. The early symptoms may be mild and non-specific. In these circumstances, many patients and, unfortunately, their doctors may simply put the changes down to 'age'. In elderly patients who are already known to be suffering from a chronic condition, the new and non-specific symptoms may be assigned to the natural progression of their already diagnosed condition. These 'creaking gates' and those who are 'failing to thrive' are difficult diagnostic problems.

Some stoical patients continue to suffer their complaint until the final stages of what transpires to be their terminal illness. These tough and determined people may not present until the cancer makes itself evident by the destruction caused by its extensive spread to other organs (secondary spread or metastatic spread, usually to the liver or bones).

Patients with known serious conditions may be unable or unwilling to undergo the extensive and sometimes unpleasant investigations that are needed to pursue a possible underlying malignancy. Examples are patients who lack insight and comprehension, due to their dementia, depression or serious difficulties in communication. Patients too short of breath to lie flat and patients with joint deformities, who lack sufficient flexibility to undergo special examinations, are also disadvantaged. However, advanced technology is gradually overcoming some of these problems.

For all of these above reasons, delayed diagnosis is unfortunately common in elderly patients. Sometimes, the delay could have been avoided, but not in all instances.

THE MANAGEMENT OF CANCER IN ELDERLY PATIENTS

Essentially, the process should be the same as with younger patients. However, modifications will be needed in some instances, because of frailty due to co-morbidity or because of patient choice.

Telling the patient the diagnosis

Most patients with cancer have a suspicion about their diagnosis from the time of their initial consultation. Most will want their fears confirmed once the diagnosis has been established. Some will prefer not to know and will deny any worries or concerns – their wishes should be respected. However, it will make the initiation of appropriate treatment difficult, if not impossible, especially where detailed patient co-operation is needed.

Some children of patients, that is, middle aged adults, will try to be over-protective. They will fear that their mother or father will be unable to cope with 'bad news'. Generally, these fears are unfounded and the elderly person will usually have already survived more psychological traumas than their children. Such anxious 'children' should be reassured and informed that competent adults (such as their parents) cannot be denied information relevant to their own well being and future management, unless they themselves express a desire to remain in ignorance.

Breaking bad news is always difficult and distressing, and it should be done in as sympathetic and empathic a way as is possible, in suitable surroundings and circumstances. However, any patient who asks an honest question has the right to receive an honest answer, however inconvenient the timing or circumstances prevailing at that time. To prevaricate may be unkind. It is not always possible or appropriate to give the whole truth in a single sitting; it may be better to reveal the information in instalments.

It is important that the information given to the patient should be well documented in the medical records. This should avoid misunderstandings and confusion in their future management. Family and friends also need to be given the same information as that being provided to the patient, unless the patient decides otherwise.

TREATMENT OF CANCER

Once the diagnosis has been made and the patient has been informed, the next step is to decide on the treatment. This will clearly depend on the patient's wishes, as well as on the site, nature and extent of the underlying malignancy. The options will be:

(a) curative surgery;

(b) radiotherapy;

(c) chemotherapy;

(d) palliative care;

(e) a combination of some of the above.

Curative surgery

This remains the first option where the lesion is accessible and there is no evidence of distant spread. To be classified as a 'cure', the patient only needs to survive for five years post-operatively. Elderly patients should not therefore be excluded from this option on the basis of age alone. Even a 90 year old patient may still have a further expectation of five more years of life if they are otherwise in good health. Informed consent to treat will be required. For this to be valid, the surgeon must be convinced that the patient is mentally competent to give such consent. Some elderly patients are skilled in concealing their early dementia and their intellectual deficiencies can only be revealed by formal psychological testing.

Radiotherapy

Although less invasive than surgery, patient co-operation and understanding is as important as it is for patients going 'under the knife'. Frail, elderly patients, who live alone or a great distance from the hospital and are dependent on ambulance transportation, may need to be admitted to hospital for treatment which would otherwise have been given on an out-patient basis. Robust, younger patients, supported by an active partner, may be more likely to be able to tolerate treatment as an out-patient.

If the elderly patient's life expectancy is under threat from other diseases, then the long term risks of high dosage treatment will be of less significance than in younger patients.

Chemotherapy

Because elderly patients have generally been excluded from experimental trials of chemotherapeutic programmes, the relevant risks and benefits that this treatment entails are often unknown. The cytotoxic drugs used are successful because of their ability to kill susceptible cells. Unfortunately, they are not as well targeted as one would desire. Other cells and systems may be vulnerable. Elderly patients with concurrent conditions may not be able to tolerate these drugs. Some chemotherapeutic agents are cardiotoxic (damaging the heart), some are nephrotoxic (damaging the kidneys) and some are neurotoxic (damaging the nervous system). Clearly, any patient already compromised with heart, kidney or neurological disease will not have the spare capacity to tolerate such side effects.

Palliative care

This is appropriate where it is accepted that the condition is beyond hope of cure or where the patient declines curative care. Surgery, radiotherapy and drugs all have contributions towards palliative care.

Surgical palliative care

This is usually carried out to relieve an obstruction, whilst leaving the causative growth untouched. Examples would be a colostomy (opening the bowel onto the surface of the abdomen, where waste is collected in an attachable bag), as well as various stents. The latter are tubes which are inserted into a duct which has been narrowed by tumour growth. Stents inserted into the oesophagus will enable a patient to continue to swallow and stents inserted into a closed pancreatic duct will relieve obstructive jaundice and the associated itching.

Palliative radiotherapy

This will shrink an offensive fungating carcinoma of the breast. It can reduce the bulk of a tumour which is causing pressure on neighbouring structures, such as the spinal cord or the trachea (windpipe).

Radiotherapy can also be very effective in relieving the pain caused by secondary deposits of tumours in bones.

Drugs in palliative care

Pain control is usually the first priority. Analgesics (painkillers) should be given on a regular basis to prevent breakthrough pain. Sufficient drugs of a sufficient strength should be given to ensure comfort, irrespective of any associated side effects. Unpleasant side effects, such as nausea, vomiting and constipation can be controlled with additional medications. If it is desirable to keep the analgesic (usually an opiate) drug at levels to avoid drowsiness, this can sometimes be achieved by potentiating the analgesic effects of a smaller dose by giving an anti-depressant drug at the same time.

If drugs cannot be taken by mouth, then injections, administered either individually or via a continuous pump, should be used. Alternative non-oral routes are suppositories (given rectally) or skin patches.

The concentration on pain control should not be at the expense of treating other symptoms, such as a cough, breathlessness, agitation, depression and itching, which may also be present.

PLACE OF DEATH: HOME OR HOSPITAL?

Although most people express a wish to die at home, in practice, this is becoming increasingly rare. Death in the UK is becoming a hospital based activity, although a minority of patients may be fortunate enough to be cared for in their terminal illness in a hospice. Increasingly, hospices concentrate on symptom control and hope to discharge patients home to die, with the support of their domiciliary services. Unfortunately, elderly patients often have no informal carers at home on whom they can rely and hospices often adopt an ageist policy to protect themselves from patients with an above average length of stay. The middle aged and middle classes seem to be over-represented amongst hospice patients.

When terminal patients are nursed in general hospital wards or nursing homes and there are difficulties in symptom control, then the outreach services of the palliative care services should be contacted and invited to assist in the individual patient's management.

PRE-MALIGNANT CONDITIONS

Some chronic diseases may, over a long period of time, develop malignant changes in the affected tissues and organs. The following are some examples.

Ulcerative colitis

A chronic inflammatory condition of the large bowel, which may undergo a malignant change. The carcinoma that arises may cause obstructive symptoms of the bowel.

Familial polyposis

An inherited condition, which initially consists of benign outgrowths in the large bowel. These polyps have the potential to turn malignant. There is usually a family history of large bowel cancer in these families.

Barratt's oesophagitis

Here, the cells lining the stomach extend upward to the lower end of the oesophagus (gullet). Symptoms include indigestion and, especially, acid reflux (heart burn), and a subsequent obstruction causes dysphagia (swallowing difficulties). The abnormal lining of the lower end of the oesophagus can develop into a malignant stricture.

Pernicious anaemia

Patients suffering from this have an atrophic gastritis, which can be the site of the later development of carcinoma of the stomach. Also, patients who have undergone a gastrectomy for peptic ulceration may, at a later date, develop a cancer in the remaining part of their stomach.

Coeliac disease

This is an atrophic immune condition of the small bowel, which is caused by gluten sensitivity (gluten is found in wheat flour). The changes which occur in the small bowel lead to malabsorption of nutrients. If the patient remains exposed to gluten, then they may develop a lymphoma of the small bowel.

Patients with the chronic conditions described above are always at risk of developing a malignant change. In the past, they were regularly reviewed with repeat investigations, for example, barium studies and an endoscopy, such as a colonoscopy. However, the evidence that this leads to early detection of change is debatable, as is the frequency at which the investigations should be repeated. It is probably more realistic that 'at risk' patients should be fully informed about potential future problems. They should then be encouraged to seek advice if their symptomatology changes in any way. That is the time when they should be re-examined and re-investigated.

OCCUPATIONAL CANCERS

Elderly patients may have been retired from full time employment for so many years that they may fail to volunteer details of their early work experience. Also, many doctors fail to make direct enquiries about previous employment. Additionally, the time that has elapsed between relevant work and the development of a malignant condition may be very long. Again, the association between the two events may be missed, especially when the occupational exposure did not occur during what the patient considers to have been their main function in life.

In some instances, especially exposure to asbestosis, the risk is also carried by the patient's family and those who merely lived in the locality of any dangerous industrial practices.

Established links had been demonstrated in the following examples:

(a) asbestos – mesothelioma of the chest;

(b) dye workers – bladder cancer;

(c) passive smokers – lung cancer;

(d) nuclear radiation – leukaemia;

(e) outdoor workers – skin cancer.

CARCINOMA OF THE PROSTATE

The prostate gland surrounds the urethra as it leaves the bladder. The gland increases in size with increasing age. If the enlargement encroaches on the lumen of the urethra, then an obstruction of urinary flow will occur. Early symptoms of prostatic enlargement are frequency and urgency of micturition (the passing of urine) and a poor stream of flow, with terminal dribbling. The enlargement of the gland is most commonly due to benign prostatic hypertrophy (BPH) and urinary obstruction is the only significant complication.

Malignant disease of the prostate also rises with increasing age, the increase starting at about 50 years of age and peaking in the 70s. The early symptoms are the same as those of BPH. If the malignancy progresses, it may spread locally into adjacent tissues and cause pain. Distant spread is mainly to the bones and these secondary lesions may or may not cause pain. The affected bone is more vulnerable to trauma and fractures may occur as a result of minimal provocation.

The first step towards diagnosis is usually a digital rectal examination. If the gland is big but smooth, then BPH is the most likely diagnosis. If areas of irregularity are felt, then the suspicion of malignancy arises. Imaging can be performed by ultrasound and a biopsy of a suspicious irregularity is also a fairly simple localised procedure (at least for urologists).

The measurement of prostatic specific antigen (PSA) is a blood test which reflects prostatic size and activity. However, there are difficulties in the interpretation of the results. There is a normal increase in levels with age and prostatic size (BPH patients have raised levels). The highest levels are found in cases of malignancy, but there are difficulties in defining reasonable cut-off levels. The test has potential as a useful screening device, but it needs more refinement than is currently available.

Treatment of cancer of the prostate is also problematic. Early cases may be best left untreated, especially if the patient has other health problems. The natural life expectancy in early and untreated cases in patients aged 70 is about 10 years. Some urologists will recommend radical prostatectomy (surgical removal of the gland) or radiotherapy in early cases. Unfortunately, serious side effects, such as impotence, may be a common complication.

Radiotherapy is the treatment of choice if local invasive spread has occurred. If there is widespread metastatic disease, for example, with bone secondaries, then hormonal therapy is recommended (flutamide and cyproterone).

Unfortunately, cancer of the prostate remains a very unpredictable condition. It may run a very indolent course or it may progress in an aggressive fashion. The extent of pain experienced is also very variable if the patient develops bony secondaries.

BREAST CANCER

About half of all cases of breast cancer occur in women over the age of 65 years and its incidence rises with increasing age.

Incidence of cancer of the breast

Women under 65 years of age	60 per 100,000
Women over 65 years of age	322 per 100,000
Women over 85 years of age	375 per 100,000

The diagnosis is usually first made by the patient on feeling a lump in one of her breasts; this should be confirmed by a biopsy. Indolent forms of carcinoma are more common in elderly patients. However, if and when metastatic spread occurs, elderly patients appear to fare far worse than their younger contemporaries.

Treatment is usually performed by the removal of the lump and axilliary glands, possibly with additional treatment with radiotherapy. Hormonal treatment with tamoxifen is accepted as beneficial. Chemotherapy in elderly patients is controversial and more research is required.

Screening by mammography in the UK stops at the age of 65. Patients can demand to continue in the programme and should be encouraged to do so.

CANCER OF THE LUNG AND BRONCHUS

This is currently twice as common in men as in women. The latter are, however, catching up, due to their acquisition of the smoking habit. It is the commonest form of cancer death in the western world.

The diagnosis must be confirmed by the examination of tissue removed during a biopsy. The method of management would depend on the nature of the malignant cells, the patient's other medical conditions and any evidence of metastatic spread. If the lesion is still localised and is sensitive to radiotherapy and/or chemotherapy, then age alone should not be used as a deterrent. Surgical removal will also depend on the nature of the cells and localisation of the lesion, but also on general lung function. This is often restricted, especially if the patient has been a lifelong smoker and their restricted respiratory reserve will prohibit drastic lung resection.

The early detection of cancer of the lung is difficult in elderly patients. Many will also be suffering from chronic obstructive pulmonary disease (chronic bronchitis) and ischaemic heart disease as a consequence of their smoking habit. These co-morbidities will also restrict the therapeutic opportunities.

COLORECTAL CANCER

This is the second most common form of cancer and the third most common cause of death from malignancy (about 18% of the total). Ninety per cent of cases are in patients over 50 years of age and the incidence rises with age, but survival rates decrease with age.

Lesions in the distal large bowel are more likely to present early with changes in bowel habits and the passing of blood with the motions. The latter may unfortunately be dismissed by both patients and doctors as being due to bleeding piles. Early detection by examination (rectal, sigmoidoscopy and colonoscopy) and imaging (a barium enema and an abdominal CT scan) are important, as a surgical cure is a possibility in early and localised cases. An abdominal CT scan is a particularly useful examination in elderly patients who cannot always co-operate because of disabilities, such as osteoarthritis of the hip, which would make the administering of a barium enema more difficult.

Lesions on the right side of the colon and in the caecum are likely to be more occult. Late presentation is more likely and may be revealed through anaemia, secondary to slow, concealed bleeding. A barium enema and/or an abdominal CT scan are likely to be the most useful investigations. The late detection may occur only when spread of the lesion has occurred and this is usually to the liver.

Anal carcinoma has the best 'cure rate', at about 66% at five years. This is because the growth makes itself apparent at an early stage. It will be easily detected on a rectal examination, either digitally or with a sigmoidoscope.

UPPER GASTROINTESTINAL CANCER

The situation here is bleak with regard to successful intervention, which is, in most cases, if at all, through surgery.

OESOPHAGEAL CANCER

In this condition, less than 10% of patients will survive five years beyond surgical intervention. Most patients are beyond attempted curative surgery at the time of presentation. The most common symptom for this is difficulty in swallowing. Surgery, however, by dilatation or by the insertion of a stent, can often provide temporary relief to symptoms. Radiotherapy is also sometimes considered as an option.

STOMACH CANCER

About 25% of the incidences of this condition can be classified as surgical cures. New or altered 'indigestion' should be taken seriously in elderly patients; this is especially true when it is associated with weight loss. Investigation will now usually be via an endoscopic gastroscopy, which allows the inside of the stomach to be viewed via a flexible fibre optic apparatus. By this method, it is not only possible to see the lesion, but also to obtain a biopsy. Simple viewing is not always good enough to differentiate between a peptic ulcer and an ulcerating cancer.

PANCREATIC CANCER

This is probably the most silent of all upper gastrointestinal malignancies; 80% of cases only present when extensive spread has already occurred. The gradual development of silent (painless) jaundice is the most common presentation. Surgical intervention is rarely possible. However, if obstructive jaundice is present, this can often be relieved by the insertion of a stent through an endoscope.

BRAIN TUMOURS

These are much more common in children than in adults. In the elderly, there is often great anxiety about missing a cerebral tumour. This is mainly because of the associated symptoms of headaches, eye problems, paralysis, fits and an altered mental state, all of which are common in old age. However, these symptoms are more likely to have a non-malignant cause, usually as a result of vascular disease or the degenerative process of Alzheimer's disease.

The incidence of brain tumours in adult life does increase with age and peaks between the ages of 60 and 75, with an incidence of 18 per 100,000. The actual incidence of brain tumours is increasing, but the reason for this is unknown.

In elderly patients, secondary brain deposits from a known or unknown primary tumour are more common than primary lesions.

Surgical treatment for primary growths will depend on the accessibility of the lesion and the general health of the patient. Palliative relief can be obtained with radiotherapy and the use of high dose steroids, such as dexamethasone, when lesions are inoperable.

The availability of a head CT examination has greatly simplified the diagnostic dilemmas that previously taxed physicians. As it becomes increasingly common for most stroke patients and newly diagnosed patients with dementia to undergo a CT examination, there should be fewer missed brain tumours in the future.

LEUKAEMIA

The leukaemias are a varied group of malignant diseases, due to an abnormal proliferation of the white blood cells in the bone marrow. Common presenting symptoms are tiredness, fatigue, recurrent infections and bleeding problems. The leukaemias are classified according to the type of white cell – myeloid or lymphocytic – and according to their aggressiveness, which may be acute or chronic.

Figure 12.3.1 Acute myeloid leukaemia

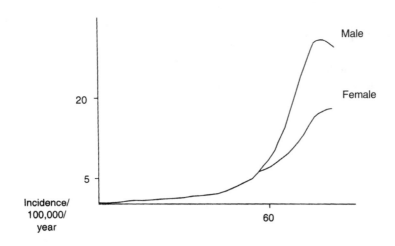

Figure 12.3.2 Acute lymphocytic leukaemia

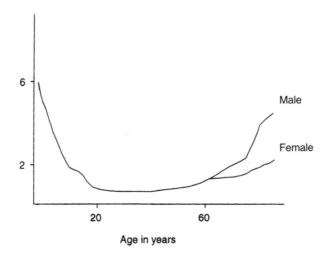

Acute leukaemias have a peak incidence after the age of 60 and they are more common in elderly people than in children (although this is not the impression one would gain from the media). In old age, acute myeloid leukaemia is more common than acute lymphocytic leukaemia. Possible precipitating factors are:

(a) a previously abnormal bone marrow;

(b) previous chemotherapy;

(c) previous radiotherapy;

(d) smoking;

(e) exposure to nuclear radiation.

Chronic lymphocytic leukaemia is almost exclusively a condition of old age and only appears in people aged over 30. It is twice as common in men than in women.

Incidence of chronic lymphocytic leukaemia

30–54 years	0.1–3.4 per 100,000
60–64 years	8.7 per 100,000
80–85 years	27.3 per 100,000

Most cases are indolent and require nothing but observation and treatment of any complications.

In acute leukaemia and aggressive forms of chronic lymphocytic leukaemia, the advice of an oncologist or clinical haematologist should be sought.

Case 19: why did it take two years to diagnose cancer?

Facts of case

A man of 76 years was referred to an out-patient clinic in September 1993. He was complaining of weight loss, possibly as much as four stones in as many months, poor appetite, dizziness and impaired mobility.

He was admitted to hospital within two weeks and was fully investigated for his weight loss. It was suspected that he had an underlying malignancy, but no evidence could be found to support this diagnosis. In particular, his peripheral blood film and biochemistry, including his liver function tests, were all normal. A barium enema showed no abnormality, neither did a gastroscopy, nor did an ultrasound of his abdomen. His dizziness and mobility were improved after simple changes to his medication and the attention of a physiotherapist. After two weeks, it was possible for him to be discharged from hospital. Unfortunately, he failed to keep his out-patient follow up appointments.

In August 1994, he was again admitted to hospital after complaining of dizziness. As on the previous occasion, adjustments to his medication and physiotherapy improved the situation and he was discharged after two weeks. Once again, there were no abnormalities in his peripheral blood film or his biochemical investigations.

In May 1995, a diagnosis of Parkinson's disease was first made and he improved with appropriate treatment.

In July 1995, he started to complain of abdominal pain and weight loss. He was once again admitted to hospital. No abnormality was found in his abdomen and his peripheral blood film was within normal limits, but there were very minor changes to his liver function tests. He was thought to be suffering from depression, was prescribed anti-depressants and, after a month, was discharged home.

Within three days, he was re-admitted to hospital as a result of a general deterioration in his condition and was said to be confused. The confusion was thought to be an acute toxic state secondary to a chest infection, which was demonstrated on a chest x-ray. With antibiotics, he improved a little. However, there was a further setback when he suffered a stroke. On this occasion, it was felt that his liver edge was just palpable below the right costal margin.

Having improved a little from his chest infection and stroke, he was re-examined after a week and, on this occasion, his liver was described as being enlarged and craggy. An ultrasound of his liver was carried out and this showed it to be full of metastatic disease. The pancreatic duct was also distended and there appeared to be an expansion of the head of the pancreas. By this time, his liver function tests were grossly abnormal.

A diagnosis of carcinoma of the pancreas was made, with metastatic spread to the liver. In view of the extensive nature of the disease, curative intervention was considered impossible and also inappropriate, because of his other co-morbidities. It was decided that palliative care alone was appropriate. The patient continued to deteriorate and died within 48 hours.

Allegations made by the family

The family complained that it was obvious that the patient had cancer from the time of his first referral in September 1993, two years before his death.

Expert opinion

From his hospital notes, it was clear that the patient was adequately investigated at the beginning of his deterioration and, clearly, there was no supportive evidence to suggest the suspicion that his doctor shared of an underlying malignancy. This continued to be the case right up until his final admission to hospital 23 months later. Only in the last month of his life did he develop abnormalities and signs suggestive of widespread malignant disease. At this time, further investigation was not possible, because of co-morbidity (his chest infection and stroke). However, when slightly improved, it was possible to carry out an ultrasound of his abdomen, which showed widespread malignant disease.

It was explained to the family that adequate steps had been taken to exclude malignant disease when he first presented and that there was no supporting evidence until immediately prior to his death. It also had to be pointed out that carcinoma of the pancreas is usually beyond curative intervention by the time that the diagnosis is made. There was, therefore, no evidence of avoidable or unreasonable delay in making his terminal diagnosis and that, even if the diagnosis had been made perhaps a month or so previously, it would still have been impossible to proceed to surgical intervention and attempted cure.

Outcome

The family accepted the explanation and did not proceed with the case.

Case 20: the occult brain tumour

Facts of case

The patient was a man of 85, who had a long history of cardiopulmonary disease, including tuberculosis. In February 1990, he collapsed whilst in a toilet. There were no witnesses to the event. On being found, there were no central nervous system abnormalities, although the patient was confused. He was admitted to hospital, where various investigations were performed to find the cause of his collapse, but nothing came to light and he was discharged.

Two months later, he was re-admitted after a further episode of collapse but, as on the previous occasion, there were no new clinical findings. A month later, there was a similar episode and again a month after that. The latter episode occurred in the hospital out-patient department, where there were many witnesses, including medical and nursing personnel. There were no reports of any involuntary movements or incontinence.

Two months later, the patient was admitted to hospital once again and, at the time of admission, he was quite rigid and it was reported that he was having 'twitching movements'. The possibility of epilepsy was considered for the first time and an electroencephalogram (EEG) was requested, which gave some support to the theory, but was inconclusive. Two weeks later, there was a further collapse and, following that episode, there were some mild left sided neurological signs. He was started on anti-convulsants but, three days after starting treatment, he had a definite, witnessed, epileptic convulsion. One week later, a head CT scan confirmed a right fronto-parietal lesion, which was thought to be a glioma. He was treated with dexamethasone. The patient was encouraged to undergo a biopsy of the lesion but, on two occasions, both he and his family refused. Two months later, they changed their opinion and a biopsy was carried out, which confirmed a poorly differentiated glioma. Following the performance of the biopsy, the patient's condition deteriorated rapidly and he died within six weeks.

Allegations made by the family

The family claimed there had been an undue delay in arriving at the correct diagnosis of the glioma.

Expert opinion

It was explained to the family that, for the first six months of his terminal illness, the patient's episodes of collapse gave no indication that would suggest a neurological cause. Because of his past history of cardiopulmonary problems, it seemed more appropriate to search for a cause in either his cardiac or respiratory systems. Once there was clear evidence of possible epilepsy, appropriate investigations were carried out within a reasonable time limit and treatment with anti-convulsants was started. When a biopsy was eventually carried out two months after the original CT scan, it unfortunately confirmed that the lesion was inoperable. The delay in carrying out the biopsy had, to a great extent, been due to the patient and his family's reluctance to proceed in that direction. Although the delay was unfortunate, this did not have any influence on the final unfortunate outcome.

Outcome

The family accepted the explanation and did not proceed with the case.

Case 21: rehabilitation blamed for patient's death from malignancy – surgeons later accepted responsibility

Facts of case

The patient was a 69 year old woman who had a 10 year history of diabetes. In the middle of August 1991, she was admitted to hospital with possible septicaemia. Coliforms were obtained from cultures of her urine and her blood cultures were negative. She responded to treatment with appropriate antibiotics. There was also concern about a possible mass in her abdomen in the left iliac fossa. This mass was confirmed to be present on an ultrasound. She went on to have a barium enema, which showed widespread diverticular disease and the possibility of malignancy in the large bowel. A flexible sigmoidoscopy failed to confirm the malignancy. The patient was also complaining of some dysphagia and an endoscopy showed an oesophageal stricture. The patient was discharged home by the middle of September.

Six weeks later, she was reviewed as an out-patient and was informed that a biopsy, taken at the time of endoscopy, showed that the specimen was benign. She was followed up in out-patients for a further six months and was then discharged.

In May 1992, she was admitted to a surgical ward because of an abdominal obstruction and an emergency caecostomy was performed. The patient was generally frail with a low haemoglobin of 8.6 and was suffering from complications from the diabetes that she was known to have had for more than 12 years. An abdominal CT scan confirmed that there was a large mass in the left iliac fossa. The surgeons were apprehensive about performing a further operation and requested the advice of a consultant geriatrician and a consultant anaesthetist. The geriatrician advised that the patient's condition following a transfusion was reasonably stable and that a laparotomy would be appropriate. The anaesthetist was apprehensive, but gave no reasons for avoiding an operation. The operation was set up, but was then cancelled at short notice, and the patient was transferred to a nearby rehabilitation hospital.

At the rehabilitation hospital, the patient continued to complain of abdominal pain. Attempts were made to contact the surgeons who had arranged the transfer for the patient to be reviewed, but without success. Three days later, the patient was seriously unwell, showing signs of an underlying sepsis. Arrangements were made for her to be transferred back to the original hospital via their Accident and Emergency department. By this time, there was a large area of cellulitis affecting the abdominal wall, with areas of necrotic tissue. The patient was taken immediately to theatre for débridement and further, similar surgery was required three days later. Unfortunately, the patient's condition continued to deteriorate and she died, having been discharged from the intensive care unit at the beginning of July 1992.

Allegations made by the family

The patient's family felt that the rehabilitation hospital was responsible for the patient's decline and ultimate death.

Expert opinion

It was explained that the management of the patient's care at the rehabilitation hospital and that the actions taken there were entirely appropriate. Unfortunately, the same could not be said from the point of view of her surgical management. An expert surgical opinion was given that the initial emergency intervention at the time of admission in May had been inadequate and a subsequent operation, as recommended by the geriatrician, would have been the correct surgical course to be taken.

Outcome

The surgeons later admitted liability and the case was settled out of court.

CHAPTER 13

ENDOCRINE AND METABOLIC DISEASES AND THEIR TREATMENT

The aim of this chapter is to highlight some of the hormonal problems that can affect elderly patients and how intervention will have both positive and negative aspects. Most people associate 'raging hormones' with youth and adolescence. Unfortunately, hormones can also rage at the other end of life but, more frequently, it is the difficulties caused by waning hormones that lead to most problems in the elderly.

The common metabolic problems of old age medicine that will be considered are:

(a) diabetes mellitus;

(b) thyroid disease;

(c) steroid abnormalities;

(d) hormone replacement therapy;

(e) the use of hormone manipulation as therapy.

DIABETES MELLITUS

Introduction

The name comes from the ancient clinical finding that the patient is passing large amounts of sweet urine. This is because their blood sugar is high. The sugar level in the blood is normally controlled by insulin, a hormone secreted by the pancreas. Diabetes in young patients is usually due to a deficient supply of insulin. This can also occur in old age but, more commonly, the insulin levels in elderly patients are high. It is the peripheral resistance and ineffective utilisation of the insulin that allows the blood glucose (sugar) level to rise in these older patients.

To have a persistently high blood sugar is undesirable, as it causes damage, especially to blood vessels. It is through the mechanism of circulatory change that diabetes mellitus causes problems. Vulnerable areas are the eye (diabetes is the commonest cause of blindness in the UK), the nervous system, the heart, the brain and the kidneys. The resulting problems are strokes, heart attacks, heart failure and kidney failure. The reduction in blood flow to the extremities is the reason why diabetes is the most common underlying problem in patients in the UK requiring amputations. In general, diabetic patients experience worse health than non-diabetics. They are more prone to infection as well as vascular disease. It has been suggested that diabetes mellitus, especially if poorly controlled, advances ageing by about 10 years. There is now good evidence that good diabetic control reduces the incidences of complications and morbidity.

Incidence

About 6% of the elderly population in the UK is known to be diabetic (higher levels are found in the Asian population). However, about another 3% of the elderly have diabetes, but it is undiagnosed. The incidence of diabetes is increasing and it also rises with increasing age. The majority (60%) of diabetics are pensioners; some will have grown old with their disease, whilst others may acquire it as a new problem in old age.

Presentation

The presentation of diabetes is less dramatic in older patients. The dramatic rapid weight loss with presentation in coma is very much a thing of the past and, even when it still occurs, it is usually in children and adolescents. The presentation in old age is usually by chance (on screening) or because it aggravates an already established medical problem or presents as a complication of the diabetic process. Failing eyesight, increasing angina, strokes and recurrent infections are all the most common mechanisms of high blood sugar levels being detected.

Treatment

The essential aims of diabetic treatment are to balance the diet against exercise and against insulin levels. All diabetics should be on a controlled carbohydrate, low fat diet – refined carbohydrate (sugar) is particularly to be avoided. In fact, a 'healthy diet' comes very close to a therapeutic diabetic diet. Elderly patients are often restricted in their exercise abilities, but the lack of extremes and their more regulated lifestyle may make control easier rather than harder.

Insulin levels may be manipulated by:

- insulin injections, if the natural insulin level is low or abnormal;
- sulphonylurea drugs to encourage a failing pancreas to produce more insulin;
- biguanide drugs, in order to enhance the peripheral action of insulin;
- drugs which reduce carbohydrate absorption.

Insulin control of diabetes

Most young diabetics require insulin injections and so do about 10–15% of older patients. The majority of elderly diabetics are controlled by diet and drugs. As a consequence, they are sometimes considered to be only 'mild diabetics'. However, this is misleading when one considers the increased health risks to which they are exposed. Whatever the nature of diabetes, its treatment or its duration, it is a serious health problem.

Many elderly diabetics who require insulin are unable to manage their own injections. Impaired vision (due to diabetic eye changes) and a lack of dexterity (sometimes as a consequence of diabetic nerve damage) are the main hindrances. In these cases, they must either depend on a relative or a district nurse to assist in drawing up the insulin and administering the injection. The process can be made easier by using fixed syringes and by storing pre-prepared syringes in the refrigerator. The situation is further complicated when it is impossible to control the blood sugar by a single daily injection. Sometimes, precision of control is sacrificed for the convenience of once daily injections – the patient must be made aware of the disadvantages as well as the benefits of such a dosage regime. Long acting insulins and mixtures of insulins can be dangerous to use in elderly patients, because of the risk of night time hypoglycaemia (low blood sugar levels); see below.

Drug control of diabetes

This is generally a more convenient form of management. Unfortunately, it will be unsuitable for patients whose diabetes is severe and is generally not advised if complications of their diabetes are severe and the symptoms are difficult to control. The progression of neuropathy or advanced peripheral ischaemia may be slowed by switching affected patients from tablets to injections of insulin.

Shorter acting drugs are preferred in elderly patients because of the risk of hypoglycaemia. Drugs with a prolonged action may accumulate and insidiously cause hypoglycaemia, especially at night. The problem may not be recognised and dismissed as being merely confusion in an elderly patient. Even if detected, it can, on occasions, be difficult to reverse. The biguanides have the advantage of not precipitating hypoglycaemia, but may cause the metabolic upset of lactic acidosis, that is, alter the acidity of the blood, especially in patients who have evidence of significant renal damage as a consequence of their disease.

The biguanides and the sulphonylureas can be successfully used in combination. Together, smaller and safer doses of each will be required.

New drugs which interfere with the absorption of carbohydrate from the bowel are now also available. They are sometimes poorly tolerated because of the bloating and diarrhoea which are recognised as side effects.

The drug regimes needed by many elderly diabetics are complicated. Not only does their blood sugar need to be controlled, but also the effects of diabetic complications, such as angina and heart failure. They may also suffer from other unrelated conditions, such as chronic obstructive airways disease or arthritis.

The principles of diabetic control are the same, irrespective of the patients age, that is, to accomplish as tight a control of blood sugar levels as a patient is willing or able to achieve. There will, therefore, be considerable variation in patients, from obsessive individuals who will adhere strictly to dietary advice and religiously check their own blood sugar levels on a regular basis, to patients who adopt a cavalier approach, with greater concern for the pleasures of today and little regard to the potential problems of the future. Elderly patients should be reminded that their future may be longer than they realise, especially if they aim at good diabetic control.

Complications

A number of difficulties can arise and some common examples are:

(a) hypoglycaemia;

(b) non-ketotic coma;

(c) times of crisis;

(d) patients with dementia.

These will now be discussed in more detail.

Hypoglycaemia

This is where the blood sugar falls to abnormally low levels. In diabetics, it is due to either too much insulin or anti-diabetic drugs having been administered, or a failure to take sufficient carbohydrate to cover the medication. Usually, the situation is clear to the patient, who will feel faint and anxious, and would normally compensate and abort an episode by taking some sugar by mouth. In some patients, the onset of hypoglycaemia may be either sudden or insidious. In either case, the patient may be unaware of the problem and fail to take diverting action. Elderly patients are particularly at risk, especially those on oral treatment. Confusion may be one of the early signs and thus thwart any compensating actions. Some drugs, such as beta-blockers, may also mask the symptoms of hypoglycaemia.

As elderly diabetic patients are also likely to have underlying vascular problems, then the dangers from hypoglycaemia are further increased. Even fit, young diabetics may experience transient neurological changes during hypoglycaemia. In patients with vascular disease, the consequences may not pass spontaneously, but may proceed to a completed stroke. Serious cardiac dysrhythmias (an erratic or irregular heart beat) may also be precipitated with dire results.

Elderly diabetic patients who live alone are particularly at risk, because of the non-availability of help during a crisis. Such patients should not be encouraged to run their blood sugars towards the lower end of the normal range; slightly higher blood sugars will be safer for these patients.

Multiple transient episodes of hypoglycaemia may lead to widespread neurological damage with impairment of higher functions, that is, the onset of dementia. Severe prolonged hypoglycaemia will lead to a coma (unconsciousness) and death. Hypoglycaemic patients are in urgent need of sugar.

Non-ketotic coma

This is due to a lack of insulin. The blood sugar rises unchecked to very high levels and the salts and acidity in the blood also become deranged. As these changes occur, the patient becomes increasingly unwell and drowsy, and will eventually fall into a coma.

In young patients, the above sequence of events may accompany an underlying infection. Ketones (which smell like pear drops or nail varnish remover) become detectable on the patient's breath and in their urine. In the non-ketotic form of coma, this does not happen and the changes in the patient may remain unrecognised. This is particularly so in elderly patients.

These patients need insulin, but elderly patients also have an even greater need for fluid replacement. Their high blood sugar and disordered salts will have lead to the passing of great volumes of urine and subsequent dehydration. Elderly patients will need urgent correction of their biochemistry, but gradual improvement is advisable, rather than dramatic reversal of the abnormalities. Frail, elderly patients are not always capable of coping with sudden change for either better or worse.

Where the episode has been triggered by an underlying infection, this will need to be detected and treated appropriately. Once elderly patients with hyper-osmolar non-ketotic coma (HONK) have been treated, it is often found that the subsequent management of their underlying diabetes is simple and modest.

Times of crisis

These occur when insulin or anti-diabetic drugs are needed, but the patient is unable to consume the compensatory amounts of food which are also required to cover the treatment. Such instances are before, during and after surgical operations, when food cannot be taken before or during investigations, for example, an endoscopy or a barium meal. Other difficult times are when oral substances cannot be tolerated because of nausea or vomiting.

In these situations, the simplest and most flexible approach is to use a 'sliding scale' of insulin administration. The patient will be managed on a drip so that fluids and sugar may be given as required. Frequent blood sugar checks will be carried out and, depending on the results, varying doses of insulin will be given.

Figure 13.1   Suggested sliding scale regime – two hourly testing

Blood glucose (mmol/l)	Insulin rate – units/hour	IV fluid
>15	6	normal saline
10–15	3	dextrose saline
5–10	1	dextrose saline
<5	0.5	dextrose saline

Once the situation has been stabilised, the patient can eat and drink and their normal diabetic management should be recommenced.

Diabetic patients with dementia

Because of the association between diabetes and vascular disease, patients with poorly controlled diabetes are at great risk from developing multi-infarct dementia. Those who have also experienced frequent and prolonged episodes of hypoglycaemia may also have accumulated considered cerebral damage.

Good diabetic control is a partnership between the patient, doctor, diabetic nurse and dietician. If the patient lacks sufficient insight to co-operate in this partnership, then the resulting control of blood sugar will be poor. Demented (and some depressed) patients may be unwilling and unable to co-operate. In such situations, it is better to compromise with higher rather than lower blood sugars, as less harm is likely to occur.

THYROID DISEASE

Introduction

The thyroid gland is situated in the front of the neck over the windpipe (trachea). It is not usually palpable, but may become enlarged. An enlarged thyroid is known as a goitre, which may be smooth or nodular to the touch. It is usually non-tender, unless there is a degree of infection, for example, thyroiditis (usually a viral infection).

The gland may become over-active – this is known as hyperthyroidism or thyrotoxicosis; under-activity is known as hypothyroidism or myxoedema. In old age, under-activity is about 10 times more common than over-activity. Both disorders are about twice as common in women as in men, although the rates begin to equalise in very old age.

Hyperthyroidism

The incidence of this disorder may rise slightly with increasing age, but still only reaches a rate of about half of one percent. The most common cause in old age is a nodular goitre, whereas, in younger patients, a smooth, uniform enlargement, known as Graves' disease, is more frequent.

Presentation of the disorder is more atypical and occult in older patients. However, the classical presentation of anxiety, weight loss, hyperactivity, muscle weakness, diarrhoea and heat intolerance can still occur. However, it is more likely that the increase in thyroid activity will present by causing a disturbance in another system.

Cardiac presentations are the most common. The increased level of the hormone thyroxine, leading to a rapid and irregular pulse rate (atrial fibrillation), may cause the patient to go into heart failure. Anxiety states, progressing to confused toxic states, are other presentations in later life. General wasting away and muscle weakness, leading to immobility and falls, are other possible presentations. A high index of suspicion is needed in all possible cases. Confirmation is usually obtained by the finding of raised thyroxine levels and a reduced thyroid stimulating hormone level (TSH). Further confirmation may be obtained from a radioactive iodine uptake test.

There are three options for treatment:

(a) drugs;

(b) radioactive iodine;

(c) surgery.

These can now be considered in more detail.

Drugs

It is best to use drugs such as carbimazole if there is any doubt about the diagnosis or if it is thought that the disturbed function is due to a transient cause, such as thyroiditis. The advantage of this is that the drugs can be stopped and their effects are not irreversible. Progress should be monitored by clinical symptoms and signs, as well as regular repetition of thyroid function tests.

Radioactive iodine

This will provide a permanent and irreversible solution to a hyperactive thyroid gland. Assessing the correct dose of iodine 131 is difficult and, as a consequence, many patients later become hypothyroid. The treatment takes about three months to be effective and, during this time, control with drugs will be required. Anxieties about the development of malignant changes following the use of radioactive iodine are unfounded and certainly so in elderly patients.

Surgery

This is rarely used in older patients. Careful pre-operative and post-operative care and supervision are needed. An exception would be if a nodule was suspected of being malignant.

Hypothyroidism

This occurs in about 5% of elderly people and the incidence is certainly much higher in the elderly than in the young. It is of gradual onset and is, therefore, difficult to detect, especially by relatives and doctors who may see the patient regularly. The general slowing down may be mistakenly put down to 'old age'. Similarly, the aches and pains, stiffness and decreased mobility, falls, constipation and cold sensitivity may also be similarly dismissed. If there is only a suspicion of myxoedema, then blood must be taken and examined. A low thyroxine level with a raised TSH, produced by the pituitary gland in an attempt to encourage the thyroid gland to create more thyroxine, will confirm the diagnosis. Many cases are due to an auto-immune process; further support of the diagnosis will be gained if thyroid antibodies are found in the patient's blood.

The condition will have taken a long time to develop. Correction of this disorder should also be leisurely. Replacement therapy with thyroxine (T4) should begin with the lowest possible dose, that is, 25 mcg. Increases should be gradual (over weeks and months) and progress should be monitored by clinical condition and repeated thyroid function tests. To rush the process may cause problems, such as the precipitation of angina or heart failure.

Myxoedema should be considered as a possible precipitating factor in patients with unexplained coma, hypothermia and dementia. Positive results are rare but, when obtained, may lead to a dramatic improvement in the clinical state and function of the patient.

STEROID ABNORMALITIES

Introduction

The steroid hormones are produced in the adrenal glands (situated on top of each of the two kidneys). Like all endocrine glands, they can become over-active or under-active. In fact, disease of these important glands is rare. The adrenal glands can be destroyed by metastatic deposits of cancer, by an auto-immune process or by infection (usually tuberculosis). They can be over-active and produce raised blood pressure, obesity and muscle weakness. These rare occurrences are dramatically over-shadowed by the problems (and the benefits) caused by the prescription of steroid drugs.

Steroids in the treatment of disease

The range of diseases in which steroids are used is wide. Most of them occur frequently in old age. Some examples are:

- asthma;
- arthritis;
- arteritis (inflamed arteries);
- inflammatory bowel disease (Crohn's disease and ulcerative colitis);
- some blood disorders.

Of these conditions, it is arteritis which is the most predominant in geriatric practice. The most common forms are giant cell arteritis and its counterpart, polymyalgia rheumatica. These conditions are identified by the symptoms of headaches and muscle aches and pains (especially on waking in the morning). It is an important diagnosis to make, as inflamed arteries are at risk of being occluded by the development of clots. The areas which are thus deprived of their blood supply are seriously damaged. Vision can be lost, whilst strokes and heart attacks may also be precipitated. The diagnosis is difficult to make, because there are no unique symptoms and no confirming blood tests (inflammatory markers, such as the erythrocyte sedimentation rate (ESR), will be raised, but this is common to many conditions).

Steroids have a very dramatic, overnight effect on symptoms. Patients are therefore often exposed to a therapeutic trial. Once on the steroids, it may be very difficult weaning them off. If they truly have polymyalgia rheumatica, then they may well, in fact, require treatment for two or more years. Similarly, the need for steroids in the other conditions listed above may also require continuous administration over many years.

In these chronic conditions, the benefits of steroids are not doubted. However, they also have their disadvantages – 'no gain without pain'. The dosage of steroids must therefore be kept as low as possible and be administered for as brief a period as possible. Very difficult judgments have to be made.

The risks of steroid treatment

The potential risks of steroid treatment are as follows:

(a) thinning of skin and bone;

(b) wasting of muscles;

(c) fluid retention;

(d) peptic ulceration;

(e) worsening of diabetes;

(f) cataract formation;

(g) increased susceptibility to infections; and

(h) suppression of natural production of steroid hormones.

Many of these problems are spontaneously part of ageing, for example, thinning of skin and thinning of the bones (osteoporosis – see Chapter 7). The bones can be protected from the effect of steroids by the prescription of bone building drugs (biphosphanates), along with the addition of extra calcium. The administration of extra vitamin D may also help. Hormone replacement therapy (HRT) may also be used in female patients. The giving of unopposed steroids in elderly patients can rarely be justified.

The prolonged use of steroids will suppress the adrenal gland, which may waste away, becoming incapable of spontaneously producing its own hormones. These are needed at times of crisis, such as during an infection. At such times, vulnerable patients will need to have their steroid dosage increased. The chronic use of steroids should never be stopped abruptly, as the patient can again be put at increased and unnecessary risk.

HORMONE REPLACEMENT THERAPY (HRT)

Increasing numbers of post-menopausal women are taking HRT, especially the affluent and the articulate. The essential hormone is oestrogen, production of which wanes after the menopause. Usually, progesterone is also given for the second half of what would be a normal monthly cycle. The progesterone may protect the uterus (womb) from undergoing malignant changes. However, the combination treatment also leads to the return of menstruation, which is unacceptable to many elderly women.

The considerable potential benefits from HRT are:

- protection of bones and skin;
- protection from vascular disease;
- protection from dementia.

Unfortunately, there may be a price to pay for the benefit of modifying the above normal ageing changes. The potential problems are:

- side effects – breast tenderness, bloating, fluid retention, nausea and flushing;
- the return of menstruation (regular vaginal bleeding);
- the possibility of malignant change, especially in the breast, uterus or ovary;
- thromboembolic episodes – deep vein thrombosis in the calf, with subsequent clots passing and damaging the lungs.

There is currently a large scale natural experiment in progress with the widespread use of HRT. Information is being collected but, at present, we do not know clearly the risk/benefit ratio of this form of hormonal manipulation.

THE USE OF HORMONE MANIPULATION

This is practised in the control of hormone dependent cancers, such as breast cancer and cancer of the prostate.

Oestrogen sensitive forms of cancer of the breast can have their oestrogen receptors blocked by tamoxifen. This may lead to regression of the primary tumour and also any secondary deposits.

Prostatic disease is probably best treated by castration, but this is not popular! As an alternative, anti-androgens are used. These are probably best for controlling symptoms, but may have little effect on the progression of the underlying prostatic pathology, being more successful in suppressing any secondary spread. Cyproterone and flutamide are the most commonly used oral preparations. Alternatives are the slightly different gonadorelin analogues, such as goserelin, which need to be given by injection. These preparations may also be used in advanced breast cancer.

CHAPTER 14

HOSPITAL AND COMMUNITY SERVICES FOR ELDERLY PEOPLE

INTRODUCTION

Although pensioners represent only 15% of the UK population, they are responsible for 42% of NHS consumption. This is because an older person is more likely to need help and social care. For many elderly people, there will be a relatively short period of heavy NHS consumption at the end of life. This is usually concentrated in the last 15 years of life, regardless of the age of death. Bigger individual consumers in health care are those who require expensive intervention in youth or middle age and then experience a long period of 'medicated survival'. However, the most expensive patients are those who require a prolonged period of long term care in an institution. For example, an elderly patient with senile dementia of the Alzheimer type may require constant care for about 10 years. If that is all in a nursing home, it will cost about £200,000 in care home fees alone at today's prices.

Community care – in one's own home – is encouraged, partly because it appears to be a cheaper option. In fact, most costs will be shouldered by family and friends, both psychologically and financially. Comprehensive community care for heavily dependent people is, in fact, an expensive option; it is normally only allowed in the UK for younger disabled people (an example of institutional ageism). Benefits such as mobility allowances are only available to people under pensionable age.

CARE IN THE COMMUNITY

This is dealt with first here, as it is the form of care experienced by most elderly people – but still only a minority. Between 94 and 95% of elderly people in the UK live in their own home. They may live alone (about 60%) or with a surviving partner, friend or other relative. The 60% who live alone are particularly vulnerable. They are generally the oldest and frailest, who need and receive the most help. However, their viability is precarious and only a minor change in health status may precipitate a crisis.

Most care in the community is provided by family and friends – informal carers. They number about six million individuals; most are middle aged or old. They save the country a fortune, but often at great expense to themselves, socially and financially, as well as in terms of their health.

Formal care in the community is meant to be a partnership between the statutory bodies – the local authority, social services and the NHS. Nowadays, there is a third partner in this marriage – the independent sector. The social services departments have gradually changed from providers of services to commissioners, the independent sector now being the main provider of practical services, such as domestic care and personal care. Domiciliary occupational therapy and social workers are about the only staff still employed directly by the local authorities. At the present time, there is no official regulation of private domiciliary services – standards and costs are therefore very variable. Three or four visits per day from a health care assistant is usually the maximum level of care allowed at subsidised rates. For example, a morning call to help with getting up, getting dressed and having breakfast, midday for toileting and lunch and evening for preparation for going to bed and final meal or snack. If a higher level of care is needed or desired, it will usually have to be paid for in full by the client. An attendance allowance may be claimed (day and night allowances are available) to assist in covering costs. Community social workers, the Citizens Advice Bureau and local Age Concern establishments are all available to advise on benefits and allowances.

Attendance at day centres and luncheon clubs may be available to housebound elderly people and may give at least temporary relief from their normal existence of being 'under house arrest'. Respite care in an institution can also be arranged for dependent clients in order to relieve informal carers who are the main or sole carer. The main point of contact for this form of help is, again, social services, and a charge is usually made.

Although 94–95% of elderly people live 'at home', only about 10% of them are in receipt of community services. Four to five per cent of elderly people live in care homes. This proportion will vary widely, depending mainly on the availability of such arrangements. Nationally, we have a very low level of institutionalisation of elderly people. Officially, even people in nursing homes and residential homes are classified as receiving community care. In all, about 500,000 elderly people are in care homes. About two-thirds of them are in residential homes and one-third are in nursing homes. The latter group is the most dependent. About one-third of elderly people in care homes are financially responsible for their own costs, as they have capital assets in excess of £16,000. Those with between £10,000 and £16,000 are charged according to a sliding scale. People with less than £10,000 are funded entirely at the expense of the public purse – this is the largest group.

The responsibility for the inspection and registration of residential homes is with the local authority; for nursing homes, it is with the local health authority. There is considerable local variation in costs, standards and the availability of placements. Anxieties about standards of care should be reported to the relevant registration authority. The reports on the regular inspections are public documents and should be available in public libraries. Each home will also be in possession of copies of their individual report.

Medical services in the community are primarily provided by the patient's GP, who has responsibility for 24 hour cover, 365 days of the year. Increasingly, the cover in unsociable hours is now devolved to a local GP co-operative. Residents in care homes should be able to retain their long standing GP, unless they have moved to a home at a great distance from their previous address. Residents should not be coerced into changing their GP for the convenience of the care home staff and its management. The GP should be supported by other members of the primary health care team, for example, community/district nurses, health care assistants, physiotherapists and sometimes health visitors; the GP should also have access to other domiciliary services, such as chiropody and dentistry. Domiciliary visits by NHS hospital consultants can be made to patients in care homes. In addition, patients can be referred by their GP to out-patient clinics and day hospitals.

HOSPITAL CARE OF ELDERLY PEOPLE

Elderly patients are found in all hospital departments, the only exceptions being paediatrics and obstetrics. The majority of medical beds are normally occupied by elderly patients and they are also well represented in surgical beds, particularly in orthopaedics, ophthalmology and urology. About 2% of the elderly population are in acute hospital beds at any time, that is, about 200,000 patients.

Mode of admission

Most medical patients admitted to hospital do so as emergencies, either via the Accident and Emergency department or as direct admissions arranged by their GP. A small minority will be admitted from a clinic as an emergency or as planned admissions. For 'cold' surgical procedures, the route is via the out-patient consultation. Emergency surgical patients follow the same routes as their medical counterparts.

'Cold' admissions should be well documented and the patient fully assessed, including psychological assessment. If special problems are anticipated, for example, relating to anaesthesia or anxieties about cardiac or respiratory status, then specialist advice should be sought as an out-patient before the planned admission.

There are special risks relating to the emergency admission of elderly patients to hospital. In the Accident and Emergency department, the patient may arrive without any available history, either because the patient is unconscious, confused or unable to speak. In these circumstances, information may be available from an onlooker; the patient's past history should be obtained over the telephone from their GP.

Long waits on hard trolleys may occur because of delays in being examined, receiving investigations (x-rays, etc) or waiting for a vacant bed. Any thin, frail, elderly patient, especially if anaemic, hypotensive or with a poor peripheral circulation, will be at increased risk of developing pressure sores (see Chapter 4). The resulting necrotic areas may take longer to resolve than the primary cause for the patient's admission.

Serious and potentially fatal pathology may be relatively silent in old age. This may mean that, on arrival, the patient may be allocated to an inappropriate triage category. Peritonitis, bowel perforation, acute myocardial infarction and septicaemia may all present in vague and undramatic ways in some elderly patients. Doctors expecting classical symptoms and signs, as in younger people, may be misled and underestimate the severity of the illness and the urgent need for intervention, with disastrous consequences. Elderly patients often cannot be diagnosed by simple methods; merely taking a history and performing an examination may be insufficient. Simple and relevant investigations may often be needed if serious and dangerous mistakes are to be avoided.

Patients directly admitted to hospital via their GPs are less likely to suffer from misdiagnosis. Their greatest risk of misadventure is delayed transportation to the hospital. Although the GP may have requested an urgent ambulance, there is often the incorrect assumption that nothing relating to elderly patients can be urgent, with the result that they tend to slip down the priority list. When the ambulance service delivers the patient to the hospital, their condition may have worsened to beyond the point of no return. Speed of admission is becoming increasingly important, as several forms of medical intervention are time limited, for example, streptokinase for an acute myocardial infarction and possibly future treatments for strokes.

Which hospital department?

However old a patient may be, they are as entitled as a younger person to receive treatment in a relevant department within a hospital.

The speciality of geriatric (or elderly care) medicine aims to provide specialist care to elderly patients, particularly those with medical, rather than surgical, problems. The latter are usually admitted to the specialist surgical department, but with geriatricians advising and assisting where necessary. It has to be admitted that most elderly patients are not cared for in the geriatric department.

The advantage of geriatric departments is that they will be staffed by people who are committed to providing the best care possible for elderly people. They will also be likely to be appropriately equipped. Ageism is rife within the NHS (including the hospital service). Departments of elderly care will do their best to counteract this prejudice. However, their opponents, who favour integrated services, will argue that the very existence of specialist units for the elderly is ageist! However, this does not seem to apply to paediatric facilities. Clearly, there are difficulties and differing opinions. Ageism is a problem and definitely exists. Again, there may be misconceptions – what seems to an outsider as an ageist decision may, in fact, be based on the complexities of the elderly patient's medical problems and co-morbidity (having several medical problems simultaneously).

Specialist departments for the elderly excel in their skills of managing patients with complex needs due to co-morbidity. They also pride themselves on having closer links with other departments, particularly those in the outside world, especially the local authority services. They therefore have a better track record of successful discharges of very frail patients.

However, any patient who is admitted to a department of medicine for the elderly should not be denied access to the facilities and opinions of other specialist services, such as cardiology and neurology.

Intermediate care

In addition to offering an acute medical service, the department of medicine for the elderly will also have facilities for rehabilitation and continuing care. Follow up services after discharge will also be available through the out-patient clinics and possibly through a day hospital. The latter caters for patients who require the services from at least two of the following disciplines: medicine, nursing, physiotherapy, occupational therapy, speech therapy and language therapy. Treatment is given to patients who are living in their own home and can be transported to the day hospital for therapy. Attendance is usually once or twice a week for a fixed period of time.

NHS continuing care facilities have recently become very limited. They are only accessed if the patient fits the local eligibility criteria. These vary from area to area and many are probably now unlawful in view of a recent court decision (*P Coughlan v North and East Devon Health Care* (1999)). NHS continuing care is essentially a palliative service. It tends to take mainly patients with chronic progressive neuro-degenerative diseases when it has been accepted that further improvement is no longer possible and the management of symptoms alone is paramount. Some health authorities no longer provide NHS continuing care beds, but will agree to fund suitable patients in private nursing homes. The current situation is unsatisfactory and fraught with hazards.

Just as a department of medicine for elderly patients should not be denied access to other departments, patients of those departments should be eligible for rehabilitation and continuing care beds whenever appropriate.

CHAPTER 15

DISCHARGE OF THE ELDERLY FROM HOSPITAL AND COMMUNITY CARE

INTRODUCTION

The National Health Service and Community Care Act 1990 and subsequent circulars from the NHS Executive have emphasised what is considered to be important in arranging the discharge of patients from hospital and in organising care in the community for those who are already living in the community. *The Hospital Discharge Workbook*, published in 1994, states that assessment of health and social needs should take place during the early stages of admission by a multi-disciplinary team, and that decisions should be made with full consultation with the patient and conveyed in the form of a written care plan to them also. Unfortunately, reality often falls short of this ideal.

RESPONSIBILITY OF CONSULTANTS IN HOSPITALS AND GPS IN COMMUNITY HOSPITALS FOR DECISIONS ON DISCHARGE

Consultants in hospitals (and GPs in community hospitals) in charge of the clinical care of the patient are responsible with other key workers, especially nurses, for deciding when a patient no longer needs acute care. Therefore, no patient can be discharged without the authority of the consultant or GP. Doctors may delegate this authority to another professional and frequently do so.

Those who may require services on discharge or placement into a residential or nursing home, or who may require continuing health care, will require multi-disciplinary assessment, involving professionals from health and social services, co-ordinated by a social worker/care manager appointed by the local authority.

Consultants in hospitals and GPs in community hospitals have to take into account the results of assessment and local eligibility criteria to make decisions on the most appropriate response to the patient's needs, after full consultation with the multi-disciplinary team – within available resources.

No patient should be discharged home until the doctors concerned have agreed and management is satisfied that everything reasonably practicable has been done to organise care that meets the needs of the patient in the community. This will take into account the physical and psychological needs of the patient.

While the patient has the right to agree or disagree with the decision made by the hospital, he cannot veto the after care plan considered by the hospital and the local authority to be appropriate; certainly, he cannot refuse to go back to the community with a package of care.

THE NATIONAL HEALTH SERVICE AND COMMUNITY CARE ACT 1990

On 1 April 1993, s 47 of National Health Service and Community Care Act 1990 came into force and placed responsibility on the local authority in relation to planning, financing, regulating and delivering community care services for vulnerable groups, including the mentally ill. This placed a duty on the local authority to carry out an assessment of a person's need for services and then to determine the provision of these services. Under s 46(3) of the National Health Service and Community Care Act 1990, community care services are defined as services which a local authority may provide or arrange to be provided under any of the following provisions:

- s 45 of the Health Services and Public Health Act 1968;
- s 21 and Sched 8 to the National Health Service Act 1977;
- s 117 of the Mental Health Act 1983 and Pt 3 of the National Assistant Act 1948.

Principles of assessment under the Community Care Act 1990

The following are the underlying principles of assessment under the Community Care Act 1990:

- the main objective is to determine the best available method of helping the individual to achieve maximum independence and control over his own life, taking into account his personal and social relationships and in consultation with his carers;
- the aim of assessment is to enable individuals to continue to live at home and, if that is not possible, entry to a residential or nursing home should be considered;
- the assessment may involve different agencies and professions and will take into account the wishes of the individual and of his carers, as well as the carers' ability to continue to provide care;
- while the specific duty for assessment is in the hands of the local authority, a single individual is responsible for ensuring that each case is dealt with effectively. The final objective of assessment is to reach a decision on the provision of services that meet the needs of individuals, taking into account what is available and affordable in order to design a suitable package of care;

- as the patient's needs may change over time, local authorities are required to monitor the individual needs and the package of care on a regular basis.

In addition to a package of care, the disabled independent person may require adaptations: hand rails, alarms, stair lifts, a range of day care, respite care or leisure facilities organised by the care manager. Lastly, those who cannot be looked after, despite the various adaptations and the package of care, may have to go into a residential or nursing home or may require continuing NHS in-patient care. Under these circumstances, the patient has a right, under the direction of choice LAC (92)27 and LAC (93)18 (circulars/guidelines from the Department of Health), to choose, within limit, cost and assessed needs, which home he moves in to. However, if a place in that particular home is not available and is unlikely to be available in the near future, it may be necessary for the patient to be discharged to another home until a place becomes available in the preferred home.

NHS RESPONSIBILITIES

NHS responsibilities for meeting continuing health care

The Department of Health, in its 1995 circular 'NHS responsibilities for meeting continuing health care needs' (HSG (95)8/LAC (95)5), outlines the services which health authorities must fund in order to meet continuing health care needs, including 'continuing in-patient care under specialist supervision in hospital or in a nursing home'.

In identifying those in need of continuing in-patient care, the circular suggests that this provision be arranged for:

(a) those with an ongoing need for regular clinical supervision (this, in the majority of cases, might be weekly or more frequently) because of the complexity or intensity of medical, nursing or other clinical care, or the need for frequent, not easily predictable, interventions that require the regular supervision of a consultant, specialist nurse or other member of the multi-disciplinary team; or

(b) those who require the routine usage of specialist health care equipment or treatments which require the supervision of specialist trained staff; or

(c) those with a rapidly degenerating or unstable condition, which means that the person will require specialist medical or nursing supervision; or

(d) those who, after acute treatment or in-patient palliative care in a hospital or hospice, are thought to have such a poor prognosis that they are likely to die in the very near future, meaning that discharge from NHS care would be inappropriate.

Both the NHS and local authorities have responsibilities for arranging and funding services to meet a patient's needs for continuing care and, for this, collaboration is essential.

PAYING FOR RESIDENTIAL AND NURSING HOME CARE

With the passing of responsibility for funding for community care to local authorities, individuals being assessed are means tested. Those with capital or savings of £16,000 or over have to meet the cost of the care until the savings or capital falls below the £16,000, when they can apply for assistance towards the care fee from their local authority (see Chapter 14).

OTHER ACTS/SECTIONS THAT INFLUENCE THE ARRANGEMENT OF SERVICES FOR OLDER PEOPLE

Section 21 of the National Assistant Act 1948

Under s 21 of the National Assistant Act 1948, local authorities were empowered to provide accommodation to a person over the age of 18 who is in need of care because of their age, illness, disability and any other circumstances, but, in April 1993, LAC (93)10 ('Approvals and directions for arrangements from 1 April 1993 under ss 21 and 29 of the National Assistance Act 1948') changed this to a *duty*.

Section 47 of the Health Service and Public Health Act 1968

Section 47 of the Health Service and Public Health Act 1968 empowers the local authority to provide services for the elderly in order to promote their welfare.

Carers (Recognition and Services) Act 1995

This Act places responsibility on local authorities to assess the needs of carers and individuals in need of community care services.

Guardianship (s 7 of the Mental Health Act 1983)

An application for guardianship may be made where a patient is incapable of making a reasoned decision and where there is conflict between the wishes of the relative and what is considered to be in the best interests of the patient. The application requires the recommendation of two medical registered physicians (one being an approved specialist). It is usually made by an approved social worker and provides the following powers to the guardian:

- the power to require the patient to reside at a specified place;
- the power to require the patient to attend places at set times for medical treatment;
- the power to require access to be given to a medical practitioner, approved social worker or other specified worker;
- the power to detain a patient in a place of safety for six months, renewable for a further six months, and then for periods of one year at a time.

People disputing discharge from NHS in-patient care to a nursing home

If, after multi-disciplinary assessment, a person is deemed not to be in need of hospital care and is offered a place in a nursing home but refuses to accept discharge, the hospital, after discussion with the relevant health authority, housing and social service department, may plan discharge to the patient's own home or alternative accommodation, with a package of care and services.

This is a last resort and involves serving a letter specifically asking the person to vacate the bed he is occupying. If this is unsuccessful, he will be considered as a trespasser and a court order will be sought to secure eviction.

Case 22: failure to ensure that services and aids were in place prior to discharge – re-admission with a hip fracture

Facts of case

An 89 year old man was admitted after being found on the floor of his bedroom by his wife. At the time of admission to hospital, he had signs of cerebrovascular accident (stroke) affecting his right arm, right leg and his speech. Prior to this, he had been diagnosed as having osteoarthritis of the knees and mild dementia. Despite these problems, he was independent in activities of daily living and he lived with his wife, with the assistance of a home help twice a week for shopping and cleaning and 'meals on wheels' five days a week.

After the completion of treatment, including rehabilitation, doctors noted that he was now more dependent, that is, he was unsteady on his feet, required a frame for walking and had difficulty getting out of a chair. He was referred to an occupational therapist and a social worker for assessment prior to discharge. The occupational therapist completed her assessment in hospital and, after performing a home visit, recommended a bath rail, a toilet surround, a commode and twice daily home care. The occupational therapist asked the social worker to organise these services and made a referral to the community occupational therapist for aid. One week later, doctors discharged the patient home but, sadly, he was re-admitted after he had fallen and fractured his right femur.

Allegations made by the family

The patient's son made a complaint to the hospital for sending his father home too soon. The hospital immediately replied, stating that his father had been fully assessed by all the relevant professionals and all the recommendations made by the occupational therapist had been followed. When the son pointed out that no aids had been placed prior to discharge, the hospital blamed this on the social services occupational therapist department.

Expert opinion

The son immediately consulted a solicitor who, in his letter, pointed out that the hospital had failed in their duty to ensure that a post-discharge plan of services and aids was in place to meet the patient's needs.

Outcome

The hospital accepted the fact that, although they had carried out multidisciplinary assessment, they had not checked that all the recommendations were in place prior to discharge. They agreed to settle out of court.

CHAPTER 16

THE PROFESSIONAL NURSE'S ACCOUNTABILITY IN RELATION TO THE CARE OF OLDER PEOPLE

Harry Kilvington, Nurse Expert Witness, BNA Consultant
RGN, Orthopaedic Nursing Certificate, Certificate in District Nursing

INTRODUCTION

Cases involving the care of the elderly in hospital and community settings occupy the vast majority of the case load on which the author is consulted.

The statutory standards for practice in the nursing profession covers all aspects of nursing practice. Frequently encountered cases are where nursing staff have failed to observe the professional guidelines. Nursing staff complying with professional requirement must be able to justify the decisions they made during the course of their practice. To practise in a safe and competent way, a registered nurse should ensure that the guidelines set by the United Kingdom Central Council for Nursing, Midwifery and Health Visitors (UKCC) have been followed and that the civil law duty of care has been complied with.

The common complications that can develop as a consequence of poor health, such as reduced mobility and a diminished ability to be independent in activities of daily living, are a potential threat to every patient. In geriatric medicine, however, the risk of developing complications is significantly increased.

Nursing is a constantly evolving profession. Increasingly, nurses are becoming autonomous practitioners. There is a corresponding increase in professional accountability for registered nurses.

STANDARDS OF CARE

When considering the standard of care provided to a patient, a court would review the care by subjecting the available evidence to the *Bolam* test. This has been defined in *Bolam v Friern Barnet Hospital Management Committee* (1957) as:

> The test is 'the standard of the ordinary skilled man exercising and professing to have that special skill. A man need not possess the highest expert skill at the risk of being found ... it is sufficient if he exercises the ordinary skill of an ordinary competent man exercising that particular art'.

The nurse's duty of care

The duty of care owed to a patient by a nurse exists by virtue of the relationship in which they come into contact. The duty varies according to individual circumstances. The standard set in law to evaluate the provision of this duty of care is reasonableness. A breach of duty occurs when an error or omission takes place. The nurse fulfils the duty of care if the care provided is reasonable in the given circumstances.

The majority of care takes place within an environment where the nurse is a team member. Each trained team member would be held to be personally and professionally accountable. There is no team liability in English law. Team leaders have a duty to ensure that the team members are competent for the role in which they are employed.

Nurses have a duty to 'decline any duties they feel unable to perform in a safe and skilled manner' (UKCC, *The Scope of Professional Practice*, June 1992, section 6.4).

Delegation of nursing tasks

Qualified nurses usually work as members of a multi-disciplinary team. They will regularly delegate nursing tasks during the course of a work shift. Most usually, these tasks will be delegated to nursing students and health care support workers.

The nurse must be satisfied that the level of skill and knowledge of the team member is appropriate to the delegated task. Accountability for the delegated task still rests with the qualified nurse.

Relatives are increasingly becoming involved in providing complex nursing tasks for patients, in both the hospital and community settings. Nurses must ensure that the patient agrees with this delegation of care and that the relatives are competent and happy to undertake the nursing tasks.

THE REGULATION OF THE NURSING PROFESSION

The United Kingdom Central Council for Nursing, Midwifery and Health Visitors (UKCC)

This is the statutory body that regulates the nursing, midwifery and health visiting professions in the public interest. The principal functions of the council are to protect the public by establishing and improving standards of training and professional conduct. The relevant regulations are defined in publications from the UKCC:

Code of Professional Conduct (UKCC, June 1992);

Standards for Records and Record Keeping (UKCC, April 1993).

Code of Professional Conduct

In this document, as issued by the UKCC, it states:

As a registered nurse, you are personally responsible for your practice and, in the exercise of your professional accountability, must:

(a) act always in such a manner as to promote and safeguard the interests and well being of patients and clients;

(b) ensure that no action or omission on your part, or within your sphere of responsibility, is detrimental to the interests, condition or safety of patients.

Standards of Records and Record Keeping

In this document, the UKCC defines the purpose of records, which is to:

... provide accurate, current, comprehensive and concise information concerning the condition and care of the patient or client and associated observations;

provide a record of any problems that arise and the action taken in response to them;

provide evidence of care required, intervention by professional practitioners, and patient or client responses;

include a record of any factors (physical, psychological or social) that appear to affect the patient or client;

record the chronology of events and the reasons for any decisions made;

support standard setting, quality assessment and audit and provide a baseline record against which improvement or deterioration may be judged.

The importance of records

The UKCC defines the effective keeping of records as a means of:

Communicating with others and describing what has been done, and observed or done.

Identifying the discrete role played by nurses in care.

[Providing] organisation, communication, and the dissemination of information among the team providing care for a patient or client.

Demonstrating the chronology of events, the factors observed and the response to care and treatment.

Demonstrating the properly considered clinical decisions relating to patient care.

Key features for records

These should be made as soon as possible after the events to which they relate, in order to:

Identify factors which jeopardise standards, or place the patient at risk.

Standards of care in a nursing home

In June 1994, the UKCC issued a report, *Standards of Nursing in Nursing Homes*. The provisions of this report included that:

Owners and matrons should ensure that staffing numbers are sufficient to allow for absences and to permit continuity of care to be achieved.

Staff should have proper training and supervision. Night staff should be included in these programmes.

Moreover, the report stated that there should be residents' charters and written standards of care. The UKCC's standards for record keeping, the administration of medicines and the code of professional conduct should all be observed.

The practice of nursing

Current practice in nursing is to plan individualised nursing for those interventions which are nurse initiated and relate to all activities of living. The plan that has been formulated relates to the clinical environment which unites the patient and the nurse.

In compiling the care plan through assessment, the following issues are incorporated: physical, psychological, socio-cultural, environmental and politico-economic.

The first phase of this assessment of the activities of living is to establish baseline information against which further information can be compared. This initial assessment should be the starting point for a care plan. The assessment process should involve:

- the collection of information from/about the patient;
- review of the information;
- identification of the problems;
- identification of the prioritisation of the problems.

The assessment and the stationery on which it is recorded are variously referred to in the nursing world as Nursing Assessment, Patient Assessment, Nursing Kardex, Nursing History and Patient Profile. ('Kardex' is a proprietary brand of a patient nursing record system. However, like the word 'Hoover', Kardex has become a nursing noun.)

Reassessment should take place whenever any significant event occurs, for example, surgery, transfer of location, following a decline or improvement in health and on receipt of relevant information.

Scope of professional practice

Historically, doctors had overall responsibility for the care of patients, although certain tasks were delegated to nurses. In 1992, *The Scope of Professional Practice* was introduced by the UKCC. This recognised that nurses have the potential to develop their role and has allowed them to undertake tasks that were previously only carried out by doctors. Now, nurses have to ensure that they maintain their competence and acknowledge any limitations. With regard to vicarious liability, employers have to approve any advancement of the nurse's role and provide the relevant education and training. Guidelines and protocols, under which the nurse will work, will also have to be ratified by the employer or relevant Health Authority. The professional standards that a registered nurse must provide apply to all areas in which a qualified nurse is employed.

Conditions requiring nursing interactions

In geriatric medicine, the provision of care may not be sharply distinct between a hospital and a community setting. The continuum of care has developed 'hospital at home' care schemes. Patients in nursing homes can receive care from qualified nurses equal to that they would have received in a hospital ward.

In all care environments, elderly patients frequently require assessment and nursing interventions to counteract the risk of developing pressure sores and to overcome incontinence.

PRESSURE SORES

Introduction

Before 1970, wounds caused by insidious trauma, pressure ischaemia or both were described by various terms/descriptions in the UK; popular terms were bed sores and decubitus ulcers. The universally accepted description applied to this clinical condition now is the term 'pressure sore'. A broad definition of a pressure sore is an area of local tissue damage which is caused by pressure, shear or friction.

Causes of pressure sore development

The main cause of pressure sore development is the application of pressure. There are, however, reasons why some patients may be more susceptible to pressure sore development than others:

- *intrinsic factors* – these include increased age, poor nutritional status, altered levels of consciousness, impaired mobility and incontinence. Other factors are concurrent disease, medication and skin conditions;
- *age* – the effect of increased age may vary between individuals. The age related factors include the loss of cushioning as a result of a reduction of subcutaneous fat, a reduction in skin elasticity, causing a lack of resilience and capacity to stretch, and a general slowing down of the tissue repair mechanism. However, pressure sores can occur even in the young, who are not affected by age related intrinsic factors.

Nutritional status

Research has shown that patients with energy/protein deficiency have a significant risk increase of developing a pressure sore. Other nutrient deficiencies thought to influence an increased pressure sore risk are vitamins and trace elements. The only factor that the research identified that was of more significance was immobility.

Ideally, pressure sore risk assessment should trigger a comprehensive dietary assessment. Where possible, the patient should be encouraged to maintain a well balanced diet. If this is not possible, nutritional supplementation, following advice from the dietician, should be implemented.

Altered loss of consciousness

This can be caused by either disease process or medication and results in the body's inability to respond to the protective stimuli, such as numbness or pain, to move the body's position. This factor extends the length of time that parts of the patient's body are exposed to pressure.

Level of mobility

The body's normal protection against pressure damage is to shift the body weight frequently throughout the day and night. Lack of mobility has been shown by research to be one of the most important contributory factors in the risk of developing pressure sores. The reduced mobility can result from many causes; the most common are pain, sedation, disease and trauma.

In these patients, frequent repositioning must be carried out in order to maintain the integrity of the skin. There is no recommended frequency for repositioning. The positioning schedule will vary from one person to another, depending on the tolerance to pressure that is determined by a combination of factors. This can only be ascertained by the examination of the skin.

Incontinence

Incontinence has been shown to be a significant predictor of pressure sore risk. Moisture, in the form of urine or perspiration, does not directly cause pressure sores, but it has been suggested that it does increase the friction on the skin. Both urine and faeces contain waste products that have chemical interactions, resulting in burning and irritation of the skin. Detailed attention to the methodology of skin cleansing is good practice in pressure sore prevention.

Medication

Both sedatives and analgesics reduce the pain sensation and hence the stimulation to move. Some blood pressure control medications, for example, hypotensive medications, result in the lowering of tissue perfusion by blood and lead to an increased susceptibility to ischaemic damage. Steroids, taken over an extended period and in high doses, have a thinning effect on the skin.

Concurrent disease

This affects a patient's likelihood of developing pressure sores, depending on the systemic manifestations of the disease process. An example of such a disease is peripheral vascular disease, where the sufferer is more likely to develop a sore on the heels.

Extrinsic factors

The three main extrinsic factors are:

- pressure;
- friction; and
- shear.

In reality, these three factors rarely occur individually.

Pressure

The application of pressure will eventually lead to the occlusion of the blood supply to the affected area. The periodic relief of pressure will restore the blood supply. By relieving the pressure, there will be a longer period of resistance to the pressure before tissue death occurs. The amount of pressure required to cause vascular occlusion varies between individuals. Most people are unaffected by a short period of high pressure but, when subjected to a sustained period of low pressure, are likely to develop a sore.

Shear

The shearing force is produced by two adjacent surfaces sliding against one another. An example of this phenomena is a patient slumped in a chair. The patient's skeleton and muscles move, while the skin does not, causing vascular occlusion as previously described.

Friction

Friction is the force generated between two surfaces, for example, the force between the bed covers and the skin. The most common cause of this is when a patient is dragged, as opposed to lifted, during repositioning.

Common sites of pressure sores

The areas most at risk depends upon the patient's position. During sitting, the majority of the body's weight is supported by the buttocks. When laying, the patient's weight is distributed more evenly over the whole of the body, resulting in lower pressure at each point.

Risk assessment

The aim of this process is to prevent the development of pressure sores. Risk calculators have been developed to assist the assessment of risk potential. There are many variants of risk calculating methods; the two most commonly used are the Norton scoring system and the Waterlow score risk assessment. The risk assessment, once evaluated, should always be followed up by a preventative action, part of which should include regular reassessment of the risk. This cannot be defined as a specific time span, but should relate to alteration of the patient's condition and/or treatment, and so will vary between intervals.

Risk assessment should be carried out on admission to any new care setting. In ill patients, it may be necessary to carry out assessment daily or even at a rate of once per shift, reflecting the frequency with which the patient's condition may change.

Risk management strategy

An organisational risk strategy should include policies and guidelines on the following: training initiatives for all staff involved in patient care, policies on pressure sore prevention, risk assessment, treatment regimes, monitoring and evaluation, policies on the provision, care of equipment and mechanisms for audit.

The risk management strategy identified for an individual patient should reflect the area of deficit identified, for example, if the patient is identified as having a poor nutritional status, the care plan should reflect that. Since the main cause of sores is attributable to pressure, every effort should be employed and reflected in the care plan to reduce the amount and duration of the pressure. This can be achieved by simple turning techniques, frequent repositioning and by the use of pressure relieving devices.

Pressure relieving devices and reducing equipment

Pressure relieving equipment

This is any dynamic system that alternately applies and relieves pressure by redistribution over a greater surface area.

The provision of such equipment should be total and not just be the provision of a specialist mattress or bed. Seating appropriate to the patient's requirements and with a correct cushion should be supplied. Other equipment, such as a monkey pole that allows a patient to lift himself to relieve pressure and bed cradles that lift the weight of the bed clothes, should be utilised.

Alternating pressure devices

These are powered devices which function by increasing the surface area in contact with the body and thus reduce the pressure at any single point. Non-powered sources are mattress overlays and provide mainly comfort. Powered systems are air filled and come in three forms: mattress overlay, mattress replacement and full bed system.

Seating

Similar equipment to that described for a bed is available for seating, although most systems are pressure reducing.

Conclusion

The conclusion to this analysis of standard pressure sore care is that prevention is better than treatment and that the principal aim of all nursing care is to prevent the development of sores. In order to achieve this, individual nurses need knowledge of the basic principles of prevention. Care providers should draw up guidelines for the management and prevention of pressure sores, with an audit process to evaluate compliance.

Good practice in the prevention of pressure sores would be to evaluate the patient through assessment using a risk assessment scoring system, ensuring all factors that affect the patient's susceptibility to the development of sores are included. The findings should be clearly documented in the records. A protocol for nursing interventions should also be included in the records. Nurses should record that the recommended actions have been followed and the result of these actions evaluated. Any equipment used to care for the patient should be mentioned in the records and the effectiveness of the equipment should be evaluated and recorded in the records regularly. The risk assessment should be repeated at regular intervals or at any time when there is a significant alteration to the patient's condition. The care provider should ensure that the information relating to the care of the patient is up to date at all times. All nursing staff should have training in pressure sore prevention.

INCONTINENCE

Introduction

Continence is a physical skill acquired from social training. The development of incontinence is symptomatic of an underlying disorder that may be mental, physical, social or environmental in its cause. The primary nursing role in assisting an incontinence sufferer is to develop interactions to promote continence whenever that is applicable.

When continence is assessed as not being attainable, the nurse's aim is to provide the highest standard of care and management to achieve independence and personal dignity to enhance the patient's quality of life.

Good practice for the management of incontinence

Good practice for the management of incontinence is to formulate a plan to promote continence. An individualised approach is required and is developed by assessing, evaluating, planning and implementing care.

There should be a collection of detailed information about the patient's incontinence before a plan can be devised. The pattern of the problem can be defined by toilet charting, which will provide baseline data for the formulation of continence plans. Information regarding fluid intake is relevant, since a low intake can result in concentrated urine, which is a bladder irritant. Other contributing factors, such as impaired mobility and/or eyesight, should be evaluated in the assessment.

Combined with the individualised care plan, it is necessary to provide the patient with bedding and body garments, formed from drainage fabrics, to protect the skin from constant urine. Penile sheaths may be applied to male patients.

Faecal incontinence requires immediate cleansing. Skin barrier creams can offer protection. The long term use of incontinence pads is not an ideal solution, as they frequently cause irritation to the skin and often fail to contain the excrement; thus, they are believed to contribute to pressure sore development. The patient's diet should be reviewed and appropriate changes should be introduced, such as a high fibre diet to help with the regulation of defaecation.

Specialised nurse practitioners, known as continence advisors, are available for consultation in most regions. These practitioners have a wide product knowledge. Where appropriate, the continence advisor would assist in developing an individual plan to promote retraining in bowel and bladder function. If retraining is evaluated as not being appropriate, incontinence aids are introduced. These can be broadly categorised as:

- absorbent or containment aids; and
- collection or conduction aids.

Maintaining a patient's dignity and privacy should be prime considerations throughout all stages of the nursing provision.

CONCLUSION

The principles of law regarding a registered nurse's liability in relation to a duty of care, and the guidelines set down by the UKCC *Code of Professional Conduct*, should be taken into account in every element of nursing care and in all caring environments.

Nurses are accountable for their practice to:

- their patient, through the common law duty of negligence;
- their employing authority for breaches of job descriptions and protocols;
- the nursing profession, through the *Code of Professional Conduct* and other UKCC professional guidelines.

The provision of quality care for the elderly involves understanding a multitude of factors that relate specifically to the ageing process, as well as factors that relate to all age groups in a caring environment. The standard of planned care should follow a dynamic standard setting system, which divides the planned care into a structured process and outcome.

The care plan should be reviewed at regular intervals, so that progress is made towards achieving the patient's defined goals. This may ultimately include 'dying with dignity'.

A professional nurse's duty of care to an older adult patient should take full account of the complexity of all influential factors. The nurse should ensure that the caring provision is regularly reviewed and that the nurse is at all times safeguarding and promoting the individual patient's well being.

Case 23: failure to prevent pressure sore development

Facts of case

Mr GM suffered from diabetes and also had a generalised arteriosclerotic condition. He had smoked 20 cigarettes a day until approximately eight weeks prior to his admission to hospital for a 'femoral-popliteal' bypass operation.

Following the operation, his leg was placed in a foam trough to stabilise the limb. The nursing records stated that Mr GM's circulation was checked every hour for the first twelve hours. The nursing records also stated that pressure areas were treated every four hours. Pressures areas were recorded on the third post operative day as being 'intact'. The next entry stated 'heel black'. Despite the discovery of the pressure sore on the heel, no further assessment of Mr GM's condition was recorded in the nursing notes.

An assessment of pressure sore risk, using a Waterlow table, had been recorded post-operatively as being 18 (very high risk). There were no further assessments recorded in the nursing records. There was no record that the nurses had attempted to use any effective pressure relieving device, even when the pressure sore was discovered, other than a ring of cotton wool with a bandage wrapped around it. The ward nurses attending Mr GM examined his toes to check his circulation, but they had failed to lift his heel from the bed and note that this was taking pressure.

The nurses provided an appropriate standard of post-operative care with regard to recording cardiovascular observations for a patient who had undergone arterial surgery. However, they had apparently failed to consider basic nursing care. Any body tissue that is subjected to continual pressure has the potential for the blood supply to that area to be impaired, with the associated threat of death of the local tissue. Mr GM's heel was subjected to continual pressure. It was immobilised; if Mr GM felt any pain, then he simply pressed the release mechanism of his patient controlled analgesia and the pain went away. Mr GM was a case of a pressure sore waiting to happen; his post-operative condition should have given the nurses a warning.

Mr GM complained to the hospital about his sore heel and received a reply that told him that the pressure sore on his heel was due to his poor blood supply and not to any lack of treatment.

However, the nursing records stated very clearly that, when they checked Mr GM's circulation every hour, they found that his toes were warm and pink. This is a sign that the operation had been a success and that Mr GM's circulation in that part of his body was not affected by a poor blood supply, but it was pressure on the heel that had caused the pressure sore. It took two years for Mr GM's pressure sore on his heel to heal completely

Outcome

Mr GM received an out of court settlement from the hospital trust.

Case 24: failure to assess patient for risk of pressure sore development

Facts of case

Mrs AB was a patient in the nursing home suffering from Alzheimer's disease. She was mainly confined to bed. There was no documentary evidence that the nursing home had carried out any assessment of her condition. There was also no documentary proof that a risk assessment had been carried out or that an assessment of her dietary needs had been undertaken. It was only after sores were visibly developing that any mention of a turning regime or of devices to relieve pressure were mentioned in the nursing records.

Despite knowing that sores had developed, the ensuing care was of a poor standard and the pressure sores worsened. The patient died.

Expert opinion

The consultant in charge of the patient's medical care gave evidence that she developed a sacral sore that measured 10 x 12 cm and a sore on her heel that had a black necrotic area and measured 8 cm square.

At the inquest into this patient's death, it was established that the open sores on the sacrum and the heel had been a significant contributory factor to her death.

Outcome

A claim for compensation was made on behalf of Mrs AB's estate for the unnecessary pain and suffering that she experienced prior to her death. It was successful.

CHAPTER 17

LIFE EXPECTANCY

ELDERLY POPULATION

All industrialised countries, including the UK, have seen dramatic changes in the population structure (see Figure 17.1) – both the proportion of elderly people in the population and the absolute number have increased dramatically from about two million in 1901 to nearly 10 million in 1990. This change has resulted from a fall in death rates in infancy and childhood from infectious diseases and a fall in the birth rate in the second half of the 20th century. Between 1981 and 1995, the percentage of 60–65 year olds dropped by three per cent, while the 75–84 group rose by 14% and the over 85 group rose by 75%. This trend is likely to continue over the next 20 years.

While the majority of those growing old are healthy and active, there is an increase in the rate of disability with age – while only 5% have problems with walking between the ages of 65 and 69, the figure rises to 47% for those over 85 years of age. This is the age group which makes the most demands on health and social services.

Figure 17.1   **Changes in population structure from 1891 to 1973 (from Coni, N, Davison, W and Webster, S, *Lecture Notes on Geriatrics*, 1977, Blackwell Scientific)**

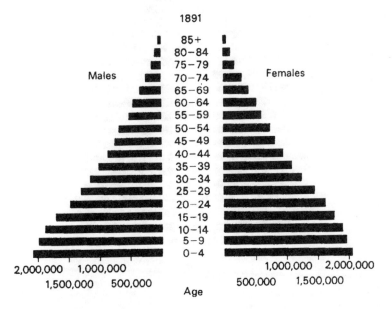

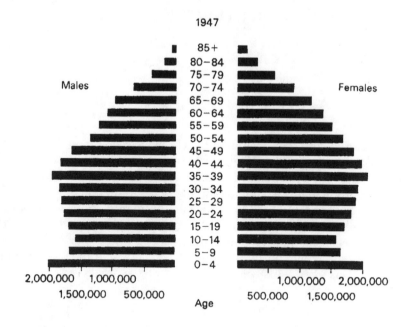

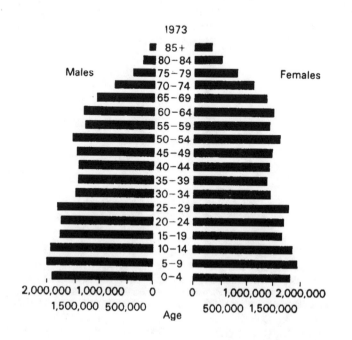

DEFINITIONS OF LIFE EXPECTANCY, LONGEVITY AND LIFESPAN

In understanding life expectancy, it is important to appreciate the differences between lifespan, longevity and life expectancy.

Longevity is the theoretical maximum length of time to which an individual of a species could survive under ideal conditions. It is usually fixed for a species and determined genetically.

Life expectancy is a predicted average (calculated mathematically) number of years an individual of a particular age can be expected to be alive and is defined by the age at which 50% of the initial population are alive. It is calculated from age specific death rates and takes into account environmental factors, but does not take into account an individual's medical condition.

Lifespan is the length of life of an individual, that is, the time between birth and death. It is variable, as it is influenced by environmental factors. Maximum lifespan is the maximum age achieved by the last surviving human being.

Life expectancy at birth

Since 1851, there has been an increase in life expectancy at birth (see Figure 17.2). While the life expectancy was 40 years in 1851, it had risen to 78.5 years by 1991. This rise has been primarily due to a reduction in mortality in infancy and childhood from infectious diseases.

Figure 17.2   Expectation of life at birth, cohort basis (from English Life Tables No 15 (1990–92))

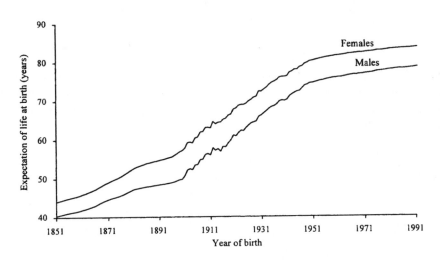

Life expectation at other ages

The figures for expectation of life at any age can be obtained from the English Life Tables No 15 (1990–92), which have been constructed using mortality figures for the population in England and Wales during the three years 1990, 1991 and 1992. Figures for selected age groups are shown in Figure 17.3, below.

Figure 17.3   Expectation of life

Age in 1991	Male	Female
0	73.4	78.9
10	64.2	69.6
15	59.3	64.7
20	54.5	59.7
25	49.7	54.8
30	44.9	49.9
35	40.1	45.1
40	35.3	40.2
45	30.7	35.5
50	26.1	30.8
55	21.9	26.4
60	17.9	22.1
65	14.3	18.1
70	11.1	14.5
75	8.6	11.2
80	6.4	8.4
85	4.8	6.1

With data from several surveys showing a decline in health and an increase in disability, a new approach has been developed to look at active life expectancy or disability free expectancy (that is, the average number of years that one can expect to live in a fully functional or 'active' state) and disabled life expectancy. In the UK, Bebbington used the data from the British General Household Survey to calculate expectation of life without disability (see Figure 17.4).

Figure 17.4   Life expectancy, active life expectancy and disabled life expectancy of men and women aged 65 years

	Life expectancy	Active life expectancy	Disabled life expectancy
Men (1976)	12.5 years	6.9 years	5.6 years
Men (1985)	13.4 years	7.7 years	5.7 years
Women (1976)	16.6 years	8.2 years	8.4 years
Women (1985)	17.5 years	8.9 years	8.6 years

However, as there are methodological problems in the calculation of disability free life expectancy, until these have been resolved and until there is a universally accepted method of calculation, it is not possible to use such a calculation in medico-legal cases.

Case 25: death during hip replacement surgery – calculation of life expectancy for the purposes of assessing the needs of the patient's husband and mother

Facts of case

A 61 year old lady (Mrs C) died during surgery for a hip replacement as a result of a drill puncturing the external iliac artery. Prior to this, she was an active individual, looking after her husband, who was 74 years of age, and her mother, who was 85 years of age. She did all her housework and prepared meals for her husband and mother, who had a dementing illness.

The solicitor who was consulted by the family asked a medical expert to prepare a report on the loss of dependency by the patient's husband and her mother and their respective needs.

Expert opinion

After an assessment of Mr C and his mother-in-law at their home, the expert noted that Mr C had ischaemic heart disease (angina) and osteoarthritis but, despite these problems, he was able to live alone in the bungalow and carry out all the basic activities, including going to the market once a week. He, however, required help with laundry, housework and cooking, activities which had been carried out by his wife prior to her death.

Mrs C's mother was dependent upon others for all her needs, except for feeding, getting in and out of bed and using the toilet.

Based on their ages, it was noted that:

(a) Mrs C (had she survived hip surgery) had a life expectancy of 22 years;

(b) Mr C, who was 74 years of age, had a life expectancy of 8.6 years;

(b) Mrs C's mother, who was 85 years of age, had a life expectancy of 6.1 years.

The expert concluded that Mrs C, had she survived, would have met the needs of Mr C and her mother throughout their calculated life expectancies.

Outcome

The hospital accepted liability for the care needs of the patient's husband and her mother for the period of their respective life expectancies. They settled out of court.

CHAPTER 18

AGE-BASED RATIONING OF HEALTH CARE

Dr Michael M Rivlin, Part Time Lecturer,
School of Philosophy, University of Leeds

At first sight, using age as a criterion for rationing is very appealing. There has to be some form of rationing in medicine. Many of the criteria currently being used for deciding the distribution of funds depend on some sort of subjective judgments. Age, it is often suggested, is objective and therefore negates the need for value judgments. Justice and fairness intuitively appear to require that finite resources be directed at the young, who have not had a chance to live their lives, rather than at the elderly, who have already lived the major part of theirs. Discussed in this chapter will be the ways in which health care is rationed in the UK. Instances of age-based rationing (ABR) will then be described (policies which deny the elderly treatment on the basis of their age) and it will be argued that such practice is both unfair and discriminatory and should not, therefore, be countenanced.

HOW HEALTH CARE IS RATIONED CURRENTLY

Rationing can be implemented in three ways: at the macro, meso and micro levels. At a macro level, rationing is determined by government directive, for instance, when ministers dictate that a drug will not be made available nationally, or as a government-community policy which excludes all those over a designated age from treatment simply because they have reached that age. Further examples of macro rationing are the denial of access to preventative medicine for elderly people as a group, even though, individually, they might benefit from it, or a policy stating that research which might help elderly patients should not be funded.

At a meso level, rationing occurs where an individual department within a hospital refuses to allow those over a certain age to be treated. An instance of this will be given shortly.

Rationing at a micro level is when a doctor acts as the 'gatekeeper' and makes the decision as to whether the patient is treated or not.

It should be emphasised that all the above methods of rationing health care can – and are – carried out either overtly or covertly. As far as macro and meso rationing are concerned, it is rare that an agency admits that it has a policy which denies patients treatment. Often, the policy is unwritten, but nevertheless enforced. On a micro level, it is unusual for doctors to tell their patients that a procedure is available but that, due to a lack of resources, the patient cannot be given it.

There are no clear principles employed by the Government to distribute funds in the NHS; rationing is implemented in haphazard ways, for instance, by postcode or by how forceful a doctor or his patient will be in demanding treatment. Another example of this inconsistency can be noted in government policy towards ABR. Although it is against government policy to permit rationing by age, ABR, as will be shown, is practised widely within the NHS.

In fairness to the Government, it would not be possible to take, for instance, a utilitarian approach to the distribution of health care. The NHS cannot be run on strictly consequentialist lines. Recently, a chief executive of one of the health authorities agreed to spend £400,000 on treating a single patient. That amount would have paid for a great many hip replacements. Was the health authority right to do allow such as decision? There is no right or wrong answer here. But, although it may be impossible to ration on the basis of clearly identifiable philosophical theories, it is essential that, at the very least, rationing decisions should be made on morally defensible grounds and the reasons behind them made public.

DO WE HAVE A LEGISLATIVE RIGHT TO TREATMENT?

Contrary to popular belief, a person has very limited legal rights to health care. GPs are not employed by the NHS but are independent contractors to the Family Heath Service Authority (FHSA). Doctors have an obligation to provide primary medical care to their patients (although it should also be remembered that a doctor can remove any patient from his panel without giving reasons to the patient for doing so) and it is their duty to provide this care regardless of cost. What primary care consists of is left to the doctor to decide. Any GP will argue that they cannot treat or care for all their patients in a way that they either want or need; there are simply not enough funds available to do so.

In a letter to *The Times*, Chris Newdick, a barrister specialising in the field of health care law, points to an anomaly in the law with regard to what GPs and health authorities are legally bound to offer patients. He notes that it is a duty of a GP to provide to their patients with '... any drugs or appliances which are needed', and 'health authorities are obliged to enforce this duty upon GPs who fail to adhere to it'. Yet, as Newdick continues, 'the [health] authorities are bound to remain within budgetary limits' (Newdick, C, 'GPs' clinical freedom in question after Viagra ruling' (1998) *The Times*, 22 September, p 23). So, it appears that a doctor has an obligation to provide drugs, even though a health authority (through the FHSA) may not be able to give him the resources to do so.

Furthermore, patients are not legally entitled to insist that services should be provided irrespective of considerations of cost. Part 1, s 1 of the National Health Service Act 1977 states that: 'It is the Secretary of State's duty to continue the promotion in England and Wales of a comprehensive health service designed to secure improvement: (a) in the physical and mental health of the people in those countries; and (b) in the prevention, diagnosis and treatment of illness.' However, Pt 2, s 1 gives power '(a) to provide such services as he considers appropriate for the discharging of any duty imposed on him by this Act'. It must be emphasised that a 'power' may be exercised, but is not normally the subject of *compulsion*. Section 3 of the Act states that 'it is the Secretary of State's duty to provide services throughout England and Wales, to such extent as he considers necessary to meet all reasonable requirements'. It will be noted that the (actual) legal onus on the Government to provide treatment is therefore so watered down as to be almost meaningless. In addition, there is also the problem of varying views as to what constitutes 'care' or 'treatment'. This is of particular relevance presently, as elderly people are being discharged from hospital into private nursing homes, for which they must pay, when (it may be argued) they are the responsibility of the State. It can be seen, therefore, that an individual's claims on the NHS may be far more limited than supposed.

DO WE REALLY PUT HEALTH HIGH ON OUR LIST OF PRIORITIES?

There are instances which show that we do not put health as high on our list of priorities as may be supposed. For instance, in the US, it has been estimated that over 50,000 deaths a year from coronary heart disease could be avoided if only a moderate amount of physical activity was undertaken (Powell, KE and Blair, SN, 'The public health burdens of sedentary living habits: theoretical but realistic estimates' (1994) 26 Medical Science Sports Exercise 851, pp 851–56). It can, therefore, legitimately be asked why people choose not to exercise (if they are able to do).

It is accepted that by buying private medical insurance one can often have an operation performed with much less delay than in the NHS. In many cases, this ability to 'jump the queue' will mean the difference between life and death for the patient. Yet, many people who have sufficient disposable income to purchase private health insurance do not do so; they decide to spend their money in other ways instead.

Of course, the public cannot be blamed for not putting health care on their list of priorities if the Government denies that rationing is necessary and some doctors continue to peddle the view that we have the best health care in the world.

ABR IN PRACTICE

That ABR policies are being implemented in some areas of medicine is beyond dispute. Sutton wrote, in 1997, 'Agesim seems to be embedded in the NHS culture' (Sutton, GC, 'Will you still need me, will you still screen me, when I'm past 64?' (1997) 315 BMJ 1032, pp 1032–33). Little appears to have changed since then; a stroke rehabilitation unit in one of the major cities, for example, does not admit anyone over the age of 65 (personal communication, 1999) and this policy is in place despite the fact that many elderly patients would benefit from treatment. As there are far more patients than places for them, some method of selection has to be made. Age is the one that is used. KM English and KS Channer ('Managing atrial fibrillation in elderly people' (1999) 318 BMJ 1088, pp 1088–89) write: 'Surveys of use of anti-coagulation show consistently that elderly people are less likely to receive anti-coagulants than younger ones on the grounds of age alone, even when the risk/benefit profile seems favourable.' What is particularly interesting about this example is that it answers those who say that age alone is never used as the reason to deny elderly people treatment.

Research by Turner et al (Turner, NJ et al, 'Cancer in old age – is it inadequately investigated and treated?' (1999) 319 BMJ 309, pp 309–12) confirms that elderly people are both under-investigated and under-treated, even though they may benefit from being treated. The authors summarise: 'Although more than a third of cancers are diagnosed in people over 75, this group is less extensively investigated and receives less treatment than younger patients.'

In the UK, old people are excluded from screening programmes for cervical cancer (Mulley, G, 'Myths of ageing' (1996) 350 Lancet 1160, pp 1160–61). Those with established cancers are less likely to be referred for specialist treatment, to be properly investigated or to receive optimum therapy. Older patients are less likely to have coronary artery bypass surgery or aortic valve replacement.

Breast cancer screening is not offered to women over 65, even though they are the very people who are most likely to fall ill with the disease (see Boer, R et al, 'Cost effectiveness of shortening screening interval or extending age range of NHS breast screening programme: computer simulation study' (1998) 317 BMJ 376, pp 376–79; Rubin, G, Garvican, L and Moss, S, 'Routine invitation of women aged 65–69 for breast cancer screening: results of first year pilot study' (1998) 317 BMJ 388, pp 388–89). Sutton writes:

> National policy in Britain is that women over 65 are not invited [for breast screening] but can be screened on request, but few women are aware of their rising risk of breast cancer with age, or of the value or availability of screening. Those who try to refer themselves face barriers and less than 2% of the eligible population are screened.

In addition to the occasions where ABR is being practised, there are other situations where it might be, but where it is difficult to be sure that it is. As an example, with regard to aortic aneurysms, 97% of all deaths occur in people over the age of 60. However, a simple and inexpensive test using ultrasound screening can easily detect those who are most at risk. If such screening were carried out, then many lives might be saved. What is the reason for not screening people, bearing in mind that tests which are performed on younger patients with different diseases may be more expensive and save fewer lives? According to Dr Malcolm Law (see Ferriman, A, 'Healthfront' (1996) Daily Telegraph, 18 November, p 62), it is because of age discrimination: 'No health minister ever gets up and says that this is the reason. But there is a lot of unspoken opposition to screening older people.'

It must be admitted that a greater proportion of elderly people are receiving complex medical treatment than ever before. As an example, it was reported that, in 1992, '12% of patients receiving kidney transplants were over the age of 75, compared to only 3% in 1982' (Parry, RG et al, 'Referral of elderly patients with severe renal failure: questionnaire survey of physicians' (1996) 313 BMJ 446). Therefore, it may be thought that the claim that the use of ABR is widespread is on weak ground. Instances such as the greater number of transplants now being performed are, of course, to be welcomed, but there is no room for complacency. Even as regards the example of elderly patients and kidney transplants, the editor of the British Medical Journal, commenting on the article by Parry et al, writes, 'Although both groups [nephrologists and physicians] seem more liberal in their attitudes than a decade ago, nephrologists remain more likely to accept certain categories of patients than physicians are to refer them. It's hard to avoid the conclusion that physicians are rationing resources – consciously or unconsciously – by patients' age' ('Editor's choice' (1996) 313 BMJ 1).

WHY ABR?

There are many justifications given for ageist policies. Some can be dismissed quite easily as being either inconsistent or fallacious. Included in these would be the following arguments that are frequently put forward.

The elderly would willingly give up their lives in favour of the young

Dr Shaw, in an article in the Journal of Medical Ethics (Shaw, B, 'In defence of ageism' (1994) 20 JME 188, pp 188–91) gives the example of a grandmother and her 20 year old granddaughter who are both drowning. He suggests the grandmother would want us to throw a lifebelt to the granddaughter in preference to herself. But the grandmother might want us to save the girl before herself because of emotional ties. The crucial test would be to find out what would be the view of the grandmother if she did not know the younger girl. It could be argued that it is stretching altruism to the limit to give up one's life for someone you don't know, and one wonders how many of us are that altruistic.

There is evidence that the elderly value their lives more highly than both their doctors, relatives and the young think they do (Evans, JG, 'Quality of life assessments and elderly people', in Hopkins, A (ed), *Measures of the Quality of Life*, 1992, Royal College of Physicians, p 109). RA Pearlman and RF Uhlmann ('Quality of life in chronic diseases: perceptions of elderly patients' (1988) 43 Journal of Gerontology M25–30), commenting on their report that elderly patients do indeed value their lives highly, write: 'Physicians should exercise caution in using their perceptions of quality of life as a consideration in medical decision making. Physicians' perceptions are skewed towards under-estimating patient quality of life.' Elderly people who are in poor health might well want to hang on to their lives when the only alternative is dying. Tsevat (Tsevat, J *et al*, 'Health values of hospitalized patients 80 years or older' (1989) 279 Journal of the American Medical Association 5, pp 371–75) confirmed that the desire to stay alive may be just as great in an older patient as in a younger one. Much more research needs to be undertaken before it can be assumed that elderly people would willingly give up their lives in favour of younger people.

Even for many of those who have reached a very old age, life is something to be valued. In a survey of 100 centenarians, selected from around the country and from various backgrounds and social classes, it was found that most have a positive attitude. When questioned on their outlook on life, '21% were wholly positive, 27% middling, with only 11% negative and 4% wholly negative' (Dally, D, *100 at 100*, 1977, Distressed Gentlefolk Aid Association). The survey concluded: 'Our overwhelming impression is of a group of individuals with great spirit and a strong will to keep going. The majority still engage with the world – travelling, studying, writing, socialising and learning new skills such as IT.'

The old will not be able to gain as much benefit from treatment as the young, as they may be physically and mentally unable to deal with the problems of old age

It has been conclusively shown that, in many cases, the elderly respond better to treatment than younger people. For instance, Vaccarino et al, analysed the data on 384,878 patients who were enrolled in the United States National Registry of Myocardial Infarction (Vaccarino, V et al, 'Sex-based differences in early mortality after myocardial infarction: National Registry of Myocardial Infarction participants' (1999) 341 New England Journal of Medicine 275, pp 275–76). They found that the mortality rates during hospitalisation were substantially higher for women than for men, and that, 'After myocardial infarction, younger women, but not older women, have higher rates of death during hospitalization than men of the same age. The younger the age of the patients, the higher the risk of death among women relative to men'.

Dr Brandstetter, referring to studies as to how elderly people cope in intensive care units, writes, 'the percentage of survivors fully recovered, freely ambulatory, fully alert and productive, was the same in the elderly (65) compared with two other age groups (41, 41–65)). Jecker and Schneiderman confirm that this is the case when they write that 'evidence is mounting that no significant age difference exists in mortality or morbidity outcomes associated with various interventions, including survival after CPR ..., coronary arteriography and coronary bypass surgery, liver and kidney transplantation, other surgeries, chemotherapy, and dialysis' (Jecker, NS and Schneiderman, LJ, 'Futility and rationing' (1992) 92 American Journal of Medicine 191). Professor Kerr, in an interview with Lois Rogers ('Doctors ban elderly patients from expensive heart surgery' (1995) The Sunday Times, 12 February, p 3), said: 'The elderly are not receiving their fair share of medical attention, partly because scarce resources are being diverted to younger patients and partly because doctors ... don't realise how much elderly patients can benefit from surgery.' There will be elderly people who might indeed not be able to cope with old age, just as some young people are not able to withstand modern day pressures, but it would be most odd if it was suggested that they be denied treatment on that basis. Many old people may thrive on being retired from work and free to occupy their days with things they enjoy doing. To suggest that the elderly do not benefit from treatment ignores research to the contrary and does not take account of differences in individuals.

Society as a whole will not gain from the treatment of the elderly, as they are likely to be both non-productive and even, perhaps, a drain on resources

(Quote from Kilner, JF, *Who Lives Who Dies? Ethical Criteria in Patient Selection*, 1990, Yale UP.) There are many groups of patients who may be considered to be non-productive, but why discriminate against the old? It is not only the old who have medical conditions that require long term treatment and where the outlook is poor. It may legitimately be asked, for instance, why we should spend funds on a younger person with a poor prognosis instead of an elderly person who could benefit far more from treatment. It must also be remembered that young patients with chronic illness may be more of a drain on resources than elderly patients, as they may have more non-productive years to live. Imagine the outcry, and rightly so, if a young paraplegic or a patient with a mental illness were to be refused treatment on this basis. If it is felt fair to refuse treatment to the old because they cannot work, consistency would dictate that we should refuse treatment to other groups of people who are also 'non-productive'.

Old age does not necessarily entail an inability to contribute to society. Here, one is not thinking only of a Picasso or a Bertrand Russell, but also the value of personal relationships between, for instance, a grandparent and grandchild. One only has to observe such a relationship in practice to realise how valuable it can be. The relationship might, in fact, be of financial benefit to the community. A paper in the British Medical Journal showed that, where a grandmother was involved in the care of child, there was less likelihood of the child being taken to an Accident and Emergency department 'with minor or trivial conditions considered not to need treatment' (Ferguson, E, Li, J and Taylor, B, 'Grandmothers' role in preventing unnecessary accident and emergency attendances: cohort study' (1998) 317 BMJ 1685).

Health care must be distributed in a way that achieves maximum benefit

(Quote from Shaw, B, 'In defence of ageism' (1994) 20 JME 188.) This is a surprising argument. If doctors decided treatment only on the basis of maximum benefit, there would be some very strange decisions made. Many of those with chronic illness, a condition with a poor prognosis or with an illness that may be expensive to deal with would not be treated at all.

Age is objective; therefore, it is not subject to the value judgments that other forms of rationing depend on

There are serious problems with this argument. First, if there were to be a policy based solely on age, then presumably there would have to be an age after which treatment would be denied. Assume that this cut-off point was decided as 65. Is it really being suggested that a heart bypass operation that might give a patient 25–30 years of good quality life be refused if the patient was a day past his 65th birthday? To those who might say that ABR could allow for this by permitting some exceptions, one could argue that this would negate the central plank of the policy. Once exceptions are allowed, then objectivity, presumably one of the principal justifications for using ABR, is removed from the equation.

Secondly, we should be clear about the distinction between chronological (or, as it is sometimes called, biological) age and biographical age. Chronological age is a person's actual age, that is, the number of years they have been alive. However, a person's chronological age may not tell us anything about them that is relevant to awarding or denying them treatment. As Coni et al write, 'It is well known that "biographical age" correlates very poorly with "chronological age"' (Coni, N, Davison, W and Webster, S, Lecture Notes on Geriatrics, 2nd edn, 1980, Blackwell). A person's biographical age is the age they regard themselves as. This is colloquially expressed as 'you are as old as you feel'. It is often biographical age that is more relevant to a patient's prognosis than chronological age and this, of course, cannot be measured objectively. For instance, a patient's attitude may be of great importance in ensuring recovery and this has little or nothing to do with their chronological age. The following anecdote illustrates well the difference between biographical and chronological age. A friend's very active 87 year old mother had been out for the day. On her return, he asked where she had been. 'Looking after an old woman of 65' she replied!

There is a another important point that must be raised with regard to both using a specific age as a cut-off point for the access to treatment and ageist policies in general. Economic pressures would inevitably ensure that, whichever age is chosen, it would soon be revised downwards. If it were established that substantial sums could be saved by denying treatment to those over a certain age, it could, and probably would, then be argued (correctly) that, by lowering that age further, even greater sums would be saved. The pressures for this to happen could be overwhelming. Of course, using age as a cut-off point will not stop some elderly people buying private care.

It must be admitted that we are not permitted to undertake certain activities until we have reached a particular age, driving and voting for instance. In view of this, it might be suggested that we do accept age as way of limiting our freedom to act as we might wish. However, it is difficult to think of examples where age would effectively condemn a person to an early death, as ABR undoubtedly would.

Having dealt with what can be considered to be the weaker arguments for ABR, detailed discussion will now move onto three arguments that arguably deserve more attention.

The 'fair innings' argument

This can be simply stated. As elderly people have lived the major portion of their lives, it is only fair that those who are younger are given preference in the distribution of scarce funds in order that they have a better chance of living theirs.

A major problem with the 'fair innings' argument is that discussion of fairness is limited to length of life. Professor Alan Maynard writes:

> The efficient use of scarce health care resources might not be the only objective of society. Society might be prepared to forego efficient health gains in order to behave 'fairly' ... One possible definition of 'fairness' in health care is that decision makers will use the NHS to reduce inequalities in people's lifetime experience of health. Such an approach reflects the idea of a 'fair innings' and could support the transfer of health gains from elderly people – who have had their 'seven score years and 10' (or, hopefully, more) – to younger people. Thus, the NHS might deny efficient treatments – such as hip replacements or coronary artery bypass grafting – to those who have had a fair innings in order to redistribute resources and inefficiently treat young, chronically ill patients [Maynard, A, 'Rationing health care: what use citizen's juries and priority committees if principles of rationing remain implicit and confused?' (1996) 313 BMJ 1499].

While one can accept that fairness is a difficult concept to define, it is difficult to discern why Maynard has chosen to use only a 'fair innings' age as an expression of what is fair in the context of the allocation of scarce health care resources. For instance, it might be considered unfair that a young drunken driver who has injured himself through reckless behaviour is preferred for treatment over an elderly person who is not to blame for his illness. A consultant in an Accident and Emergency department remarked to a friend that he was fed up with patients having to wait hours for treatment as a result of the department being full of young people who had been badly hurt due to their heavy drinking. Further, why should it be considered fair to prefer the younger person in a situation where there are two claimants for treatment, one aged 25 and the other aged 75, the former already having received a large amount of health care resources as a result of his anti-social behaviour, the latter, due to living a responsible lifestyle, having never before had to call on the NHS, but then, at an advanced age, needing the hip replacement to which Maynard refers?

One should also question the idea that, as the old have had their lives, fairness dictates that the young should be given the chance to have theirs. What is so special about the young and, in particular, *all* the young. Consider the following example. A young 'joyrider' who has just killed three people in a car crash is brought into casualty, critically ill. At the same time, the remaining survivor of the car he had hit also arrives in casualty. The survivor is known to the hospital staff as a leading consultant oncologist, aged 68, who is working on important research. Those who advocate ABR argue that the distribution of treatment must seen to be just and that health care must be distributed in a way that achieves maximum benefit. On both these counts, some might ask why the younger joyrider be given preferential treatment over the elderly physician. I am not, for one moment, advocating that we should give, or deny, treatment based on our views of the worth of an individual; the consequences of doing so are morally abhorrent and far too dangerous. As can be seen, it is an implied part of an ageist policy that the allocation of funds should be distributed in favour of the young. But what is there about being young that entitles them to preferential treatment? Surely not just the fact that they are young?

It is expensive to treat the old and the large amounts of money and resources that are spent looking after them could be better utilised elsewhere

This argument is based on a fundamental misunderstanding. The major costs of treating the elderly are not in the use of sophisticated technology, but in routine treatment and, particularly, caring. Daniel Callahan, in his important book, *Setting Limits: Medical Goals in an Ageing Society* (1987, Simon & Schuster), dealt with ABR in depth. Callahan suggested that expensive and 'high tech' treatment should be denied to the elderly and the money saved used instead on better care which would result in the old having a more meaningful life. An opposite view is given by NG Levensky in 'Age as a criterion for rationing' ((1990) 322 New England Journal of Medicine 25, pp 1813–15). Levensky writes: 'Contrary to conventional wisdom, the savings will be small if we eliminate intensive, high technology care for the aged ... For substantial savings, we must withhold routine medical care from the elderly.' Severe Alzheimer's disease patients can be hospitalised for many years. They are not subject to high tech treatment, but it is very expensive to look after them. It is the routine care (and less expensive treatments) that takes up the great majority of funds used to look after the old. Levensky showed that research in the US indicated that 'probably no more than 1 or 2% of the national health care expenditure for the elderly is devoted to high cost medical admissions'. However, whether anyone, young or old, should be given very expensive treatment that uses up large amounts of finite resources is a different debate.

Old age and dying are a natural part of life and we should not pretend, by treating death only as an enemy, that this is not the case

One can have some sympathy with this point of view. But, although intuitively the argument seems to have substance, there are two major flaws in it. First, Shakespeare said 'We owe God a life', but Shakespeare did not say when God should collect. 'When', in terms of life expectancy, is being put further off all the time. Even ignoring the rise in life expectancy due to the discovery of antibiotics, there has been, and still is, a significant upward trend in the life expectancy of the population in many of the developed countries of the world. A female born in 1993 in Japan can expect to live to 83, and future advances in science increase this even further. How can we, therefore, talk of a natural lifespan? Is the life expectancy, and natural lifespan, of a woman living in Uganda to be always, as it is now, 43? It is by treating death as an enemy that we have been able to increase both the quantity and, of course, the quality of people's lives.

Secondly, surely one of the aims of medicine *is* to interfere with what is described as the natural order of things. As Harry Lesser, in his entry 'Ageism' in the *Encyclopaedia of Applied Ethics*, writes:

> ... all medicine is an interference with natural processes, and this in itself is morally neutral. It is, in the opinion of many, inhumane and unjust to keep an elderly person alive artificially at the cost of much suffering to that person against his or her will. However, to restore them, even artificially, to what they may find a worthwhile existence is neither inhumane nor unjust. The distinction between right and wrong, or justified and unjustified, cannot rest on whether a thing is natural or unnatural, even supposing that the distinction between natural and artificial can be made, particularly in a species for whom the use of artefacts is natural [Lesser, AH, 'Ageism', in Chadwick, R (ed), *Encyclopaedia of Applied Ethics*, Vol 1, 1998, Academic Press, pp 87–94].

Within a few years, there will be over 100,000 people celebrating their 100th birthday in the US alone. The medical profession can have an important impact on how long we live and, as a result, death can be postponed for many years.

SUMMARY

One of the major problems facing doctors is that they are being forced to make rationing decisions on behalf of the Government, sometimes against the best interests of their patients. These decisions are usually made covertly and without the patient being informed that treatment is being denied because of lack of resources. (How can a patient protest about something if he is unaware that it is happening?) If society decides that age should be the determining factor as to whether a person is denied treatment, then this must be made explicit by the Government, not left to the medical profession to disguise by way of euphemisms. Only when it is admitted that ABR exists will it be possible to have a meaningful debate about the subject.

While it is not recommended that all elderly people should receive treatment, irrespective of their prognosis, age should not be used as a criterion to gain, or deny, access to medical facilities. There are obvious situations where it is the medically correct decision to refuse a person treatment because they will not be able to benefit from it. Under these circumstances, it is important to note that treatment should be denied only if it is medically inappropriate and not because of a patient's age. The inevitable consequence of an ageist policy would be to consider the old expendable, something that is surely morally unacceptable. ABR demeans our society. Unless, and until, better arguments for it are put forward, it is important that the old are not unfairly discriminated against and the policy is not given further credibility.

It might be said that, if one argues against ABR, an alternative form of patient selection should be offered. However, it is not the duty of critics of the policy to propose an alternative form of rationing. It can presumably be acceptable to show the flaws in an argument without having to suggest what to put in its place. For instance, in June 1999, there was an outcry when it was found that a hospital in Sheffield had acceded to the demands of an organ donor that his kidney should only be given to a person of white race. On hearing of this, the Government and the BMA said that this could not be allowed to happen in the future, even if it meant that people who needed transplants died as a result. The reasoning was that some things are so ethically indefensible that they cannot be countenanced, even if it does mean people dying.

CHAPTER 19

THE ROLE OF THE OCCUPATIONAL THERAPIST IN RELATION TO OLDER PEOPLE

*Tim Barnes, MA, DipC, OT, State Registered
Occupational Therapist, Rehabilitation Consultant*

INTRODUCTION – DEFINITION OF OCCUPATIONAL THERAPY

The following definition is taken from the College of Occupational Therapists' *Directory of Private Practitioners*:

> Occupational therapy is the treatment of people with physical or psychiatric illness or disability through specific selected occupation for the purpose of enabling individuals to reach their *maximum level of function and independence in all aspects of life*. The occupational therapist assesses the physical, psychological and social functions of the individual, identifies areas of dysfunction and involves the individual in a structured programme of activity to overcome disability. The activities selected will relate to *the consumer's personal, social, cultural and economic needs* and will reflect the environmental factors which govern his or her life [emphasis added].

OCCUPATIONAL THERAPY TRAINING AND FOCUS

The training for occupational therapy is a three year full time course to graduate level and includes a substantial grounding in physiology, anatomy, medicine, orthopaedics and psychiatry. Thus, an occupational therapist starts from a good general knowledge of medical matters. However, the occupational therapist is not primarily concerned with organic pathology or even with cognitive impairment. These simply form the backdrop which helps to inform the occupational therapist's assessment of an individual's functional performance. The occupational therapist's core concern is *to minimise the effect of pathology or impairment on the totality of an individual's life* – including personal and domestic roles, employment, social relationships and citizen roles. Occupational therapists will use a wide variety of tools to achieve the desired end. The choice of interventions will be determined by the individual situation.

OCCUPATIONAL THERAPY FOR OLDER PEOPLE

From the point of view of the occupational therapist, older people do not have very different needs from the rest of the population. It is perhaps more important with older people than with the rest of the population to consider their particular world view, because, almost by definition, it will be more firmly established than that of younger people. Half a century or more of adult life almost guarantees a wealth of likes and dislikes, strengths and weaknesses, firm opinions and strong beliefs. An experienced occupational therapist will always take particular account of these in working with older people, but the full range of treatment approaches and skills described later in this chapter is as relevant to older people as to the general population.

Occupational therapists working with older people do, nonetheless, frequently encounter particular problems requiring their professional intervention. Some of these problems relate to medical conditions which are common in older people, while others relate to circumstances and to functional problems which are common in older people. Examples include the following.

Osteoarthritis, rheumatoid arthritis and other joint problems

Occupational therapists will be involved in teaching individuals protective techniques, as well as providing suitable assistive equipment.

Osteoporosis, falls and hip fractures

Occupational therapists will be involved in risk management, ensuring that suitable assistive equipment is provided and used correctly, and instructing individuals and their carers in protective and recovery techniques.

Dementia and confusion

Occupational therapists have a major role in 'reality orientation', often finding that the individual will function much better within his own home environment than on a hospital ward. Interventions include the establishment of routines and suitable prompts and targeted care assistance to minimise risk and provide encouragement and support. Older people are more vulnerable than the general population to confusion arising from environmental dislocation and, particularly, from hospital admission after trauma. The occupational therapist will often be the key assessor of the individual's capacity to remain independent in his own home and the assistance required.

Housing adaptations

Older people often require some changes to their property, or a move to single storey accommodation, due to the frailty of normal aging, and any injury or specific disease process will often precipitate this need. Occupational therapists have a key role in determining the needs and, frequently, specifying the adaptation required.

The right to die at home

The right to die at home encapsulates some of the hardest dilemmas faced by occupational therapists working with older people. There is often a conflict between the 'medical' view of the world and that of the individual. With increasing numbers of very elderly and frail people living at home by themselves, there is often a serious risk attached to an elderly person returning home after a hospital admission resulting from a fall or other accident. Where an individual is determined to return home against all advice, it is most commonly an occupational therapist within the hospital or social services team who will advocate their right to do so and who will shoulder responsibility for events thereafter – often including further falls or other fatal accidents. Members of the legal profession will be well aware of the potential legal complexities in this area, but perhaps less aware that it is very often occupational therapists working with older people, together with colleagues in the community nursing services, who have to do the best they can in often very difficult and distressing circumstances.

AREAS COVERED BY A FULL OCCUPATIONAL THERAPY ASSESSMENT

Introduction

In order to achieve any measure of success, occupational therapists have to consider a wide range of factors. They have to be aware of the individual's condition: they need to understand the underlying pathology – either the disease process or the structural damage. They need to understand the progression of this condition and the available methods of medical treatment, and to have as clear a picture as possible of the longer term prognosis, taking account, for example, of the benefits and drawbacks of relevant medication. They need to understand clearly the practical and functional implications of the condition. This would involve, for example, being aware of the actions of the main muscle groups and the nerves that supply them; understanding the circulatory system of heart, veins and arteries; and understanding the skeletal system and the movements possible at every joint. In particular, therapists need to be aware of the potential for recovery, re-learning or substitution in any given condition.

Therapists also need to be aware of all types of prosthetics (artificial limbs), orthoses (splints and other devices protecting, supporting, and otherwise rendering more functional, the movable parts of the body) and all other assistive medical devices which can improve effective function. These devices are often employed at a very early stage of treatment and will often be as much a part of medical treatment as they are functional aids.

However, all this detailed information is only one parameter amongst many that the occupational therapist has to consider. The medical and immediate functional implications of disease or injury may have little or no correlation with the impact on a particular individual's life. Take, for example, a building worker in his 20s, married with small children, who suffers a spinal injury and is paralysed from the waist down. One can immediately see that he has not only lost his previous work role and earning capacity, but his family roles as father and husband have been severely compromised. Imagine now the same injury happening to a university lecturer in his 40s, who is a single man living alone. His earning capacity may not be affected at all, while the problems he will experience at home may be severe, but will be quite different.

Thus, the therapist has to understand the social and work situation of the individual being assessed, in order to understand the priorities for that individual. Equally important are the individual's personal interests and hobbies, which are often the key to motivation and engagement in rehabilitation.

Factors related to personality and psychology

A key area to which the therapist must pay attention is the personality of the individual. No amount of objective assessment will lead to any successful intervention unless the person themselves is a willing and active partner in the enterprise. The occupational therapist can only achieve results by working within such an active partnership; a failure to establish this will severely limit the effectiveness of any treatments. For many people, the greatest hurdle in moving on from serious illness or injury lies in the mind. Whatever the situation, the psychological make up of the affected individual is central to any assessment and management by the therapist. At one end of the scale, some resilient individuals who suffer catastrophic injuries which devastate their lives are able to re-orient themselves and find ways of moving on in their lives with little help from any professional. At the other end, many people who suffer comparatively minor illness or disability will 'go to pieces', losing all self-confidence and motivation, and suffering intractable depression. Therapists have to be competent to assess the psychological issues, identify depression, anxiety and other mental states that form part of the complex of issues to be addressed for a given individual. In fact, occupational therapists have a major role within psychiatry and the roots of the profession can be traced to this specialism. Many occupational therapists specialise in the field of mental health and continue working in this field throughout their careers. Their role in assessing the functional implications of mental health problems and deciding on necessary treatment parallels that in the field of physical medicine.

Environmental factors

Finally, the therapist must be aware of the physical environment within which the individual lives and works. Thinking of our building labourer and lecturer briefly described above, it is self-evident that, if the former lives in a standard semi-detached, two storey house, and the other lives in university lodgings on the ground floor, they will have different degrees of difficulty in returning to their previous home environment. The same will apply if one lives in a flat area and another lives in a hilly area. If one previously drove a car, while the other drove a motorbike – or cycled everywhere – their needs following injury will again be different.

It should be clear that an occupational therapy assessment logically starts with the individual, not the medical condition. This is particularly relevant to the medico-legal context, where the aim of returning the individual to his previous situation is an explicitly desired outcome. The following diagram may be a useful brief guide to the various categories of background information about the individual that the occupational therapist will consider within his assessment.

Figure 19.1   Background information for assessment

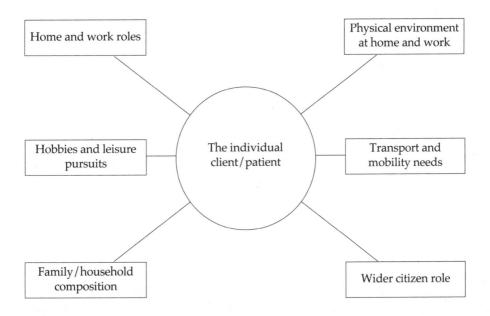

The nature of the impairment

Having gathered such baseline information, the occupational therapist will then need to consider the nature of the injury or medical condition, including the prognosis and any anticipated future medical treatment. As already stated, the focus is a strictly functional one. A useful term here is 'impairment', defined by the World Health Organisation (*International Classification of Impairments, Diseases and Handicaps: A Manual of Classifications Relating to Consequences of Diseases* (IDIDH-2), 1980, WHO) as 'problems in body functions or structure as a significant deviation or loss', caused by an illness or injury. Examples of such problems would include:

- absence of a body part;
- reductions in strength or range of movement (ROM) of a limb;
- pain (constant or on movement);
- sensory impairment;
- psychiatric condition such as post-traumatic stress disorder (PTSD) or depression;
- brain injury.

The assessment process

The occupational therapist will generally assess the functional implications of such impairments against a range of simple personal and domestic activities of daily living (ADL).

Examples of personal activities of daily living (PADL) include:

- dressing;
- washing;
- use of toilet;
- eating;
- walking;
- getting on/off bed and chair.

Examples of domestic or instrumental activities of daily living (DADL or IADL) include:

- cooking/washing up;
- cleaning/tidying;
- lifting/carrying;
- ironing;
- managing finances;
- time management.

Assessment methods will generally include direct observation of task performance and will consider all factors (physical, psychological and environmental) affecting the outcome.

The list of possible activities is endless and will be tailored to the individual occupational therapist's frequently used reference checklists, of which the Barthel Index is the best established (see Appendix 1 and, for example, Murdock, C, 'A critical evaluation of the Barthel Index Part 1' (1992) 55(3) British Journal of Occupational Therapists 109, pp 109–11; and 'A critical evaluation of the Barthel Index Part 2' (1992) 55(4) British Journal of Occupational Therapists 153, pp 153–56). However, these are increasingly being replaced by the use of standardised assessment tools, such as the assessment of motor and process skills (AMPS, see Appendix 2 and Fisher, AG, *Assessment of Motor and Process Skills*, 3rd edn, 1999, Three Star), which offer established validity and reliability for outcome measurement. The AMPS makes use of sophisticated statistical analysis and a very large sample population to provide a generalised rating of functional (motor and process) ability from an assessment of specific task performance. This enables a computer-generated report, indicating the individual's overall abilities relative to a cut-off point at which they are likely to require significant assistance with daily living tasks, as shown in Appendix 2.

Having established a baseline of functional performance, the occupational therapist will then need to consider this in respect to all aspects of the individual's life. This will almost always involve a 'home visit' to consider the immediate environmental issues and also to collect further information from family members. Assessment of the work environment should also be a necessary part of this process but, regrettably, is not commonly undertaken in the UK (see p 199 on typical work situations).

Beyond home and work – which, in themselves, can present an enormous variety of interesting challenges – the therapist will need to consider leisure activities, holidays and any other circumstances in the individual's life that may affect the interventions needed. Therapists need to be particularly aware of, and sensitive to, religious, ethnic or cultural issues, as well as individual sexuality and gender orientation.

It is impossible to capture, in a brief chapter such as this, the breadth of information that an occupational therapist can have to cover in an assessment. There is quite literally no area of life that is unimportant, or that can be assumed to be unimportant, without assessment. Unlike all other health professionals, their focus is on the subjective experience of the individual, rather than the illness or injury. This means that therapists routinely need to learn about the lifestyles, work routines and leisure activities of the people they work with – it does not take a great deal of imagination to see how wide and often extraordinary such a canvas can be! Even within the assessment process, before any intervention, there is a critical need for good social skills on the part of the therapist, who often has to delve into the most intimate aspects of life with individuals who are at their most vulnerable. Assessment sessions can be very emotional, as they often form the individual's first opportunity to express what the experience of illness or disability means to him in the context of his own life. This is so particularly when assessments are carried out in the home environment. Thus, the assessment process is, in itself, quite a significant intervention, since it is often the first point at which the individual starts to contemplate the longer term future and to come to terms with the challenges ahead for them.

TYPES OF TREATMENT

By the time an initial assessment is completed, an experienced therapist will usually have a clear picture of the types of intervention that will be most effective with any given individual, and these will be only a small subset of the possible options.

The word 'treatment' is used in this chapter because, from the viewpoint of the legal system, the essential outcome of *treatment*, whatever the word itself is taken to mean, is to restore the person as nearly as possible to the situation they were in prior to illness or injury. This outcome is sought equally by all health professionals. However, it is important to understand – and, hopefully, this will be clear from the discussion so far – that there is a significant difference between *medical treatment*, targeted at particular physical or psychiatric conditions, and more broadly based *treatment*, aimed at the restoration of optimum function and independence for individuals disabled through serious illness or injury. Indeed, there is a fundamental potential contradiction between the 'objective', mechanistic and reductionist nature of the medical science which underlies medical treatment, and the subjective, phenomenological world view in which the occupational therapist pays attention to the needs and priorities of an individual. Put at its simplest, medical science may define an injury as trivial, and individual experience may define it as catastrophic.

Without dwelling on this debate, there are two points of relevance to the current discussion. First, case history in the area of personal injury litigation in the UK illustrates quite clearly that the concept of returning an individual to the situation in which he was before the accident has been applied to that individual's entire world view, rather than to the narrowly defined medical consequences. While it is perhaps not surprising that there is frequently a conflict in evidence between doctors presenting a standardised 'diagnostic' view of an injury and an occupational therapist presenting a detailed picture of actual consequences for a specific individual, it is usually the latter that will inform decisions on the quantum of each claim.

Secondly, the debate has a fundamental relevance to the nature of treatment as practised by occupational therapists. If a strictly 'medical' and mechanistic view is taken of injury and function, it follows that a given injury can be remedied to a certain extent by, for example, assistive equipment, environmental adaptations and specific skills training, but this view does not allow for other routes to greater function. As we all know, motivation, preference, confidence and determination can all make us achieve more and better than their absence. The experienced occupational therapist will always be looking for blocks – such as low self-confidence – or keys – such as a particular favourite activity – that critically affect function. Remove the block, or tap into the key, and the physical organism functions better in his environment. This approach to assessment is particularly helpful when there are suggestions of under-performance or malingering in the case of compensation claimants; the occupational therapist is very likely to identify any discrepancies and inconsistencies in performance and draw attention to these if no satisfactory explanation can be found during the assessment.

Figure 19.2   **A diagrammatic representation of the conceptual approach upon which the AMPS functional assessment is based, incorporating many of the factors underpinning problem assessment and treatment choice (from Fisher, AG,** *Assessment of Motor and Process Skills***, 3rd edn, 1999, Three Star)**

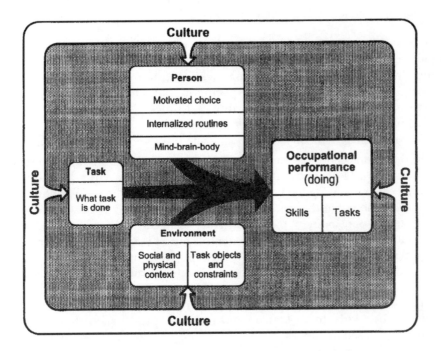

Thus, the key point about occupational therapy 'treatment' is that *any meaningful activity is intrinsically therapeutic,* increasing confidence and self-esteem and increasing the motivation to achieve more. The perfect treatment outcome would be the replacement of a vicious circle of disability, depression and loss of motivation with a benign cycle of achievement, self-confidence and ambition. Any intervention on the part of the occupational therapist which facilitates meaningful activity can thus be described as *treatment.*

There follows a brief list of the main types of interventions that occupational therapists commonly use. Further details of these models may be found in Rosemary Hagedorn's textbook (Hagedorn, R, *Foundations for Practice in Occupational Therapy,* 2nd edn, 1997, Churchill Livingstone):

- *biomechanical model* – including exercise and graded ADL programmes, compensatory equipment and housing adaptations;
- *neurodevelopmental model* – including corrective positioning, sensory stimulation and bilateral activity;
- *cognitive perceptual model* – including intensive practice, feedback, task re-learning, cueing and prompting (mainly in brain injury);
- *behavioural modification model* – including conditioning and reinforcment techniques;
- *the cognitive behavioural model* – including 'reality testing', stress management and relaxation techniques.

The use of these and other treatments by occupational therapists varies enormously depending on where they work: it is likely that only a minority of specialists working with particular well defined client groups would consciously choose to work to a specific model. Others will work more eclectically, using different tools at different times. Occupational therapists working with older people, other than those working with particular conditions such as dementia, are very likely to use a wide range of techniques.

In the next section, the work situations of occupational therapists both in this country and abroad will be considered, and this will go some way towards contextualising the types of treatment described above. For now, it is sufficient to note that there is an essential division in the UK between 'health care' – the responsibility of the NHS – and 'social care' – the responsibility of local authority social services departments. Thus, it is, unfortunately, unlikely that there will be continuity of involvement from one practitioner for all occupational therapy treatment. As an individual moves from the 'acute', 'medical' stage of illness or disability when they are an in-patient or out-patient to the 'chronic' stage when they are under the care of their GP, they will also be likely to be transferred from hospital-based therapists to community-based therapists.

TYPICAL WORK SITUATIONS

The background

It is sadly the case that there are few, if any, circumstances in the UK where sufficient funding is available to enable occupational therapists to provide the comprehensive service suggested by the definition given at the start of this chapter. As will be seen by the brief descriptions below, occupational therapists employed within the statutory sectors are limited in their role by resource constraints, the legislative mandates of their various employers and the specialist focus of their particular work situation. Nevertheless, work situations and local practice vary widely, so the following descriptions should be taken only as a general guide.

In the NHS, occupational therapists are employed in general hospitals, psychiatric hospitals, as members of community teams within mental health, learning difficulty and physical 're-ablement' or rehabilitation. In the larger hospitals, occupational therapists may work generically across all areas or be attached to particular departments. Within the health service, there are a number of areas where occupational therapists have a significant role and have built up specialist skills, including:

- neurology and spinal injury;
- upper limb injury and functional splinting;
- prosthetics and wheelchairs;
- care of older people;
- terminal care;
- paediatrics;
- learning difficulty;
- mental health;
- rheumatology.

The common theme is that occupational therapists become involved where there is a long term problem and in situations, such as the care of older people, where hospital treatment must be followed through into the home environment.

Occupational therapists are also widely employed by local authority social services departments to implement the provisions of social care legislation, including:

- the National Assistance Act 1948;
- the Chronically Sick and Disabled Act 1972;
- the Disabled Persons Act 1983;

- various Housing Acts;
- the National Health Service and Community Care Act 1992.

While this is not the place to detail the provisions of this legislation, it is necessary to point out that it predominantly concerns the social needs of individuals, rather than their health care needs. While occupational therapists working in local authority social services departments tend to focus on the biomechanical approaches described above, together with the arrangement of residual care assistance, other methods of treatment are seen as a 'health' responsibility. However, it is generally true to say that, in any given area, there will be established lines of communication and co-operation between therapists working in the two sectors. At the time of writing, the promotion by central government of inter-agency co-operation and Joint Investment Plans (JIPs), together with the increasing funding role of Primary Care Trusts, seems likely to lead to fewer 'handover problems' in the future.

Current trends

In some ways, the role of the occupational therapist in the UK has recently become wider than that overseas. An important role of particular relevance to medico-legal work is the widespread introduction, following the 1992 National Health Service and Community Care Act, of 'care management' within social services departments. Before 1992, many social services departments operated separate home care, social work and occupational therapy services, with the inevitable result that social care services were fragmented and resources unevenly distributed. 'Care management' was a model proposed, whereby one officer took overall responsibility for the services to a particular social services client. The effect of this has been to considerably increase the involvement of many social services occupational therapists in the arrangement of care assistance for the people with whom they are working, particularly those with severe disabilities. While, in some areas, this has merely clarified what was existing practice, in others, it has constituted a significant new duty for some practitioners. While occupational therapists have always had a role in identifying the tasks where an individual would require assistance, they are now commonly responsible for quantifying this assistance, commissioning it and monitoring its adequacy over time.

It is generally true that, in recent times, occupational therapists in the UK have been less involved with work rehabilitation than their colleagues overseas. While there is a small but growing independent sector of occupational therapists working on contract for insurance companies or other organisations focusing on work resettlement, this area has only recently returned to political favour, after a long period when high levels of general unemployment effectively deterred investment. There are signs that occupational therapists are beginning to reclaim this area of work, particularly through initiatives such as the launch in 1999 of the government sponsored 'New Deal for Disabled People'. In other countries, such as the USA, Canada and Australia, occupational therapists have a recognised role in carrying rehabilitation through into the workplace, where they perform work capacity assessments, undertake worksite evaluations and are involved in job analysis and redesign (Fenton, S and Gagnon, P, 'Evaluation of work and productive activities: work performance assessment measures', in Niestadt, ME and Crepeau, EB, *Willard and Spackman's Occupational Therapy*, 9th edn, 1998, Lippincott, Chapter 15, section 2). This role extends to medico-legal assessments in those countries (Morgan, AL, 'Occupational therapists in the witness box – how will we be judged?'(1999) 39 World Federation of Occupational Therapy Bulletin 17, pp 17–24).

These developments and the experience gained through them will enable occupational therapists, particularly those with social services experience, to provide comprehensive medico-legal reports covering a substantial part of the typical schedule of special damages.

Case 26: physical and psychological consequences of RTA – assessment carried out 27 months after the accident revealed significant disabilities

The report for this case was based on a standardised structure covering the following areas:

- background information;
- assessment of functional limitation;
- evaluation of:
  - past, present, and future care;
  - additional transport needs;
  - specialist equipment needs;
  - miscellaneous needs;
  - housing recommendations.

The following format can be adapted as necessary to reflect the needs of each individual claimant.

Sex and marital status:	Male widower
Age:	79 years
Previous health:	Good
Accident details:	While disembarking from bus, the door closed prematurely, trapping his arm and causing him to fall onto the pavement. His arm was trapped and then crushed by the wheel of the bus.

Treatment: Several operations to clean and repair the wound over a 10 week period, with difficulties in the eradication of deep seated bone infection. Initial suspicions of a fractured neck of left femur were proved incorrect, but the pelvis and hip were badly bruised. He was hospitalised for five months.

Time between accident and assessment: Twenty-seven months

At the time of the visit, Mr A was living with his son, who was a taxi driver. All arrangements for the visit had been made with his son, who had agreed to be present for the interview.

The background papers provided for the assessment included one medical report which described Mr A's circumstances prior to the accident accurately, in that he had lived in private sheltered accommodation some 300 yards from his son's house. However, a second report gave a very different picture. This report described an old cottage in the country, with low beamed ceilings, a spiral staircase, dogs and cats and annual visits to his son's farm, where he looked after the chickens, dogs and horses!

Instructions from the solicitor had included the comment that Mr A was 'somewhat confused'. However, there was no psychiatric or psychological evidence, and neither surgeon who had reported had mentioned this confusion. Mr A's son, in his statement, mentioned only his physical problems and his constant need for care – which, in themselves, did not 'add up'.

Thus, on this occasion, it was not clear what would be found on assessment. Mr A seemed to be well oriented – he knew where he was and understood who the assessor was and why he was there. He was quite articulate about his physical capacities and residual problems. However, as the assessment progressed, it became clear that all was not quite as it seemed. First, Mr A's description of what he could do turned out to be very different from the reality. After he explained that he could walk around the house with his frame without any difficulty, he was asked to demonstrate this ability. It was immediately obvious that his limit was a few steps and that he could not, in fact, walk any distance safely without a helper at hand to assist his balance. Mr A had scars on his forehead, which his son explained were the result of one of many falls he had had since his operation, for some of which he had required hospital admission.

Mr A's right elbow and forearm remained infected with a deep seated osteomyelitis (infection of the bone marrow) and he was wearing a dressing on this. His son explained that this dressing was changed by the community nursing service every morning. Movement in his right elbow was limited and he could neither straighten nor fully flex the joint. He had very limited movement in both shoulders.

As the interview progressed and these physical limitations became evident, Mr A became increasingly upset. When he was asked about his life before the accident, he started to give a confused amalgam of the two stories described above. His son explained that his father had indeed lived in an old cottage some 10 years before the accident and that all the circumstances he had described to the examining surgeon were accurate at that time. With the assistance of his son, Mr A's memory of his sheltered flat in which he had lived for eight years was gently explored. Gradually, Mr A became able to talk about his life there, accurately describing his patio and the plants he enjoyed looking after. He became very tearful, repeating again and again – as he had done frequently during the interview – that he wanted to go home. His son was visibly agitated whenever this subject came up.

Mr A's son was then asked to describe their daily routine. He explained that his father had stayed with him since the accident and that, immediately following discharge, Mr A had fallen while the son was out working. This had repeatedly happened, despite all the son's arrangements and admonitions. He felt that his father frequently 'forgot' how frail he was and that he was hopelessly over-ambitious in what he thought he could do. Their current routine was as follows:

4.00 am	Mr A's son would get up, bring his father a cup of tea and go to work.
7.30 am	The local authority social services department home carer would arrive, help Mr A to wash and dress and would make his breakfast. The home carer would then help him to get from his bed (in a small conservatory on the ground floor) to his chair in the sitting room and would leave about 8.15 am.
8.30 am	The community nurse would arrive to clean and dress the infected arm, and would then leave between 9.00 and 9.30 am.
10.30 am	Mr A would return from work, having done any necessary shopping on the way, and then attend on his father for the remainder of the 24 hours.

Mr A's son reported that he was unable to go to work on one day in four, because his father would be too upset for him to leave. He also said that he had started to suffer high blood pressure since the accident. Throughout the interview, he was almost as agitated as his father and was clearly extremely stressed about the whole situation. He acknowledged that he was having difficulty coping with the situation, and said that the local social services department had helped him to arrange two periods when his father went into residential care to give him a break.

Occupational therapist's conclusions and recommendations

It was clear that the accident had been a very traumatic experience for Mr A. Prior to his accident, he had been living independently, regularly choosing to travel by bus to the city centre to shop – as he had been doing on the day of the accident. He had no support at home, and it became clear on a subsequent visit to his house that the housing was only 'sheltered' in a minimal way, with the warden making one visit per day to each flat and offering no practical assistance to residents.

It was equally clear that, more than two years after this accident, Mr A remained substantially physically disabled, but, perhaps more importantly, was showing some very worrying signs of emotional disturbance, confusion and forgetfulness, which had not been present before the accident. In the absence of any other factors, this could only be attributed to the accident and its aftermath. Mr A had spent a considerable time in hospital and had undergone surgery several times. Although the focus of medical involvement had been on his physical problems, by the date of assessment, the psychological difficulties were dominant and presented the greatest challenge in terms of restoring to Mr A and his son some normality and quality of life.

There were a number of positive features in the situation. Mr A's son was clearly devoted to him. His son had no wife or children and a flexible job which allowed him to fit his work around his father's needs. Although he was clearly under great stress, there was no reason to believe that his underlying health was not reasonably good. He lived only a few hundred yards from his father's flat, which, despite his father's residence in his house, he had maintained and was available for him when circumstances allowed him to return. The flat was on the ground floor, but had only one bedroom and an awkward entrance hall with two steps to the front door. However, there were some suitable two bedroomed ground floor flats in the same development. It was also possible that his existing flat could be redesigned to improve the access and incorporate a second bedroom for a carer.

Mr A was very keen to return to his own home. At first sight, this seemed out of the question, particularly since his son was completely against the idea. At the same time, it was clear that his son could not continue caring for him without considerable risk to his own physical and mental health.

There was no doubt that Mr A would need constant supervision in the future. The history given amply showed the risks inherent in leaving him even for a short time. It was later confirmed that, during his two periods of residential care, attempts had been made by staff to improve his mobility and to increase his awareness of the danger of falls, but these had not succeeded or, in fact, made any noticeable impact whatsoever.

The main recommendation was that Mr A should return to his own home, if it could be suitably adapted, or to another flat in the same development. He would need continuous care during daytime hours and a carer sleeping in his flat who was available to provide help at night when necessary. This care would have to be provided by an agency, since arrangements had to be completely reliable. It was clear that his son could act as his advocate in terms of ensuring that suitable carers were provided for him and that he was happy with all arrangements. The cost of such arrangements, based on a sample of major agencies throughout the UK, would be in excess of £30,000 per annum.

In line with the above, Mr A's son's care to date was valued as equivalent to a residential carer.

Providing such constant attendance would not, of course, adequately compensate Mr A for his losses due to the accident. However, it would provide the basis for other opportunities. Since his accident, the necessary presence of carers for safety reasons had undermined his efforts to achieve some degree of personal independence. He was particularly upset that he was unable to dress himself – mainly due to lack of mobility in his shoulders – and was very excited when he was shown pictures of some simple dressing aids that he could use. He had not been able to make himself a cup of tea because he could not lift the kettle, so the suggestion of a 'kettle tipper', combined with the use of a light plastic jug for filling the kettle, again opened up new possibilities for him. These things might seem trivial – and in cost terms they are – but they are often of enormous importance in providing people with some personal dignity, extending their independent range of action and, with it, their confidence and self-esteem. An annual allowance for small equipment of this nature was recommended and the report included full details of relevant companies and demonstration centres.

Mr A had also been unable to visit the shops as he had enjoyed doing previously. This was mainly because he had difficulty getting into and out of his son's car and also because the NHS wheelchair that he had been given was heavy and difficult for his son to manoeuvre. Most of all, it was because his son was too worn out and worried that it never occurred to him to take his father out! Ironically, as a taxi driver, he was well aware that there was a good local wheelchair accessible taxi service, and costs were included for regular trips into town using this service. The purchase of a lightweight wheelchair was also recommended.

Finally, the report included a number of minor recommendations as follows:
- heating costs (for the past and to settlement only). Before the accident, Mr A's son was out at work all day, by his own admission, regularly working 12 or 14 hours per day, during which time his house was unheated. From the moment his father came to stay, his heating was on almost constantly, even during the summer. Mr A was able to produce a sample of bills showing the increased costs and payment of these was recommended;

- carer's costs: in the future, Mr A would have a carer always in the house with him. He would have to equip a room for the carer's use and meet a variety of incidental living expenses. Illustrative costs for these were provided;
- although it was not strictly within the remit of the report, the solicitor's attention was drawn to the loss of earnings experienced by Mr A's son while he was caring for his father. As described above, he was managing to work only about six hours per day for five days per week – about half the amount he had been working previously.

CONCLUSION

This chapter has dealt briefly with a large amount of material. The task of assessing the consequences of personal injury and recommending suitable interventions is never a simple one. The historical development of the various heads of special damages that are now generally accepted in legal proceedings owes much to the involvement of occupational therapists, who have been the first professionals to carry out comprehensive and detailed assessments of the wider consequences of personal injury. In many instances in the past, occupational therapists have been the professionals who have had to deal with the consequences of inadequate settlements and inappropriate advice. It is hoped that a growing number of solicitors working in this field now understand the value of obtaining expert reports from occupational therapists, which can provide a firm foundation for the schedule of special damages.

APPENDIX 1 – BARTHEL INDEX

General notes

The index should be used as a record of what a patient does, NOT as a record of *what a patient could do.*

The main aim is to establish *degree of independence from any help,* physical or verbal, however minor and for whatever reason.

The need for *supervision* renders the patient NOT independent.

A patient's performance should be established *using the best available evidence.* Asking the patient, friend / relatives and nurses will be the usual source, but direct observation and common sense are also important. However, *direct testing is not needed.*

Usually the performance over the preceding 24–48 hours is important, but occasionally longer periods will be relevant.

Unconscious patients should score '0' throughout, even if not yet incontinent.

Middle categories imply that the patient supplies *more than 50% of the effort.*

Use of aides to be independent *is allowed.*

Function	Score	Description Date				
Bowels in preceding week	0	Incontinent (or needs to be given enema)				
	1	Occasional accident (once a week)				
	2	Continent				
Bladder in preceding week	0	Incontinent, or catheterised and unable to manage				
	1	Occasional accident (max once per 24 hours)				
	2	Continent (for more than seven days)				
Grooming	0	Needs help with personal care: face, hair, teeth, shave				
	1	Independent (implements provided)				
Toilet use	0	Dependent				
	1	Needs some help but can so something alone				
	2	Independent (on and off, wiping, dressing)				
Feeding	0	Unable				
	1	Needs help in cutting, spreading butter, etc				
	2	Independent (food provided within reach)				
Transfer	0	Unable – no sitting balance				
	1	Major help (physical, one or two people), can sit				
	2	Minor help (verbal or physical)				
	3	Independent				
Mobility	0	Immobile				
	1	Wheelchair independent, including corners, etc				
	2	Walks with help if one person (verbal or physical)				
	3	Independent				
Dressing	0	Dependent				
	1	Needs help but can do about half unaided				
	2	Independent (including buttons, zips, laces, etc)				
Stairs	0	Unable				
	1	Needs help (verbal, physical, carrying aid)				
	2	Independent up and down				
Bathing	0	Dependent				
	1	Independent (Bath times, gets in and out unsupervised and wash self. Shower supervised / unaided)				

APPENDIX 2 – AMPS SKILL ITEMS

Motor and process skills defined in the assessment of motor and process skills (from Fisher, AG, *Assessment of Motor and Process Skills*, 3rd edn, 1999, Three Star)

Motor skills

Stabilises	Co-ordinates	Lifts
Aligns	Manipulates	Calibrates
Positions	Flows	Grips
Walks	Moves	Endures
Reaches	Transports	Paces
Bends		

Process skills

Paces	Initiates	Restores
Attends	Continues	Navigates
Chooses	Sequences	Notices/responds
Uses	Terminates	Accommodates
Handles	Searches/locates	Adjusts
Heeds	Gathers	Benefits
Inquires	Organises	

Assessment of motor and process skills graphic report (from Fisher, AG, *Assessment of Motor and Process Skills*, 3rd edn, 1999, Three Star)

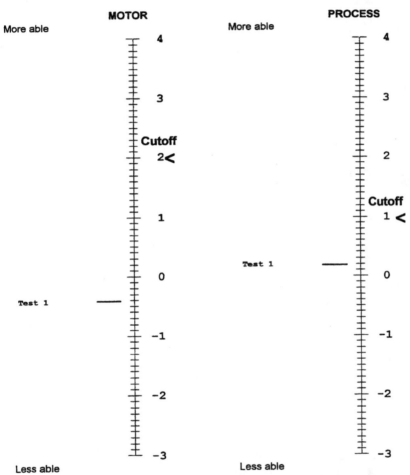

ADL motor and ADL process ability measures are plotted in reference to the AMPS scale cutoff measures. Ability measures below these cutoff measures indicate that there were problems that impacted the quality and effectiveness of performance.

	DATE	MOTOR	PROCESS
Test 1	11/13/1998	-0.4	0.2

INDEX